A FATHER'S MEMOIR

Sean Left Quietly

HENRY BLUMBERG

LINDIWE LEGACY
PRESS INC.
TORONTO, ONTARIO

PUBLISHED BY LINDIWE LEGACY PRESS INC.

Published in 2022 by Lindiwe Legacy Press Inc., Toronto.

Library and Archives Canada Cataloguing in Publication

Blumberg, Henry, author

Sean Left Quietly: A Father's Memoir

Issued in print and electronic formats.

ISBN 978-1-7781389-0-4 (paperback)

ISBN 978-1-7781389-2-8 (hardcover)

ISBN 978-1-7781389-1-1 (ebook)

1. Blumberg, Henry. 2. Blumberg, Henry—Death and burial. 3. Suicide victims—Canada—

Biography. 4. Suicide—Psychological aspects. I. Title.

Book design by Laura Boyle Design

"You, Henry are witness not only to your and Marcia's loss but to that of your father and the effects of devastating trauma on the generations that followed him.

That you are witness and now scribe allows the hidden to become heard and once it has a name it can be taken out and placed at a distance, where at best it can be understood."

—Adrian Kohler and Basil Jones. Co-Founders Handspring Puppet Company, Cape Town, South Africa

"Your memoir is very moving and profound, permeated with your warm heart. Your sorrow is real, but always you place others in the forefront, and you give prominence to the positive and the creative."

—Tim Huisamen, Lecturer in Afrikaans & Netherlandic Studies, Makhanda (Grahamstown), South Africa

"This is a story that is deeply meaningful to those who never pictured themselves in the same position, who do not know where to turn, or who don't know how to reckon with the fallout and the changes to family, let alone to the inner life."

—Susan Scott, Editor Body & Soul, Ontario, Canada

"A true labour of love which will have great relevance and meaning for all those who have suffered loss of any kind, and for all those privileged enough to read it."

—Deborah Gibson. English Teacher, Stratford, Canada.

"Your book is a beautiful tribute to Sean and to your family. It is poignant, affecting and moving. And your style, cadence and use of language are lovely throughout."

—Frances Latchford. Associate Professor, School of Gender, Sexuality, & Women's Studies, York University, Toronto, Canada

"Anyone who feels pain will benefit from this exquisite healing tool."

—Danusia (KIRN KAUR) Szwejkowska. Yogi, Artist, and Healer, Toronto, Canada

In memory of Sean

In the recesses of my mind, I kept hoping that early one morning, standing on the deck of our Muskoka cottage, watching the dark sky turn pink over the lake, I would see our canoe gliding slowly out of the receding grey mist—and there would be Sean, paddling back to us.

Rational thinking cannot compete with such yearning.

CONTENTS

FOREWORD

In August 2012, just as he was boarding an overnight flight back to Toronto, Henry Blumberg received a call telling him his youngest son had taken his own life. As the plane hurtled across the dark Atlantic, Henry, unable to process what he had nevertheless long dreaded, thought of his own father. As a child, Julius Blumberg had been sent to America from Latvia with an aunt. He did not then know he would never see his parents again, though they knew the sight of the young boy in short pants walking up the gangplank into an uncertain future could be their last. Henry imagined his grandparents watching their child disappear from sight as he flew home anticipating the same.

This memoir from a grieving father, written over a period of ten years after his son died by suicide, offers a way not only to live with the loss but also to transform it into a part of oneself. This way is not methodical or simple: it requires courage, retrospection and deep effort. Most of all, it requires empathy and generosity and a willingness to be re-wounded when all the broken spirit wants is to curl inward to numbness. There are no phases of grief to be passed through, only the hard task of working through trauma, of reviewing all of one's own life and the life of the deceased, knowing there will be no final resolution. But there will be a shifting, a movement that clears room and accommodates the pain as part of the self, forever altered as understanding is gained.

What is this understanding and how is it grasped? The memoir shows us that understanding does not mean getting to the root cause of the suicide, tracing all the signs—though this search is unavoidable. Acts of remembrance are essential as rites of connection. But the deepest understanding is a hard-won knowledge of who his son was, and this knowledge is starkly transformative. It is transformative because the effort to understand requires looking unblinkingly at the complex context of this act of desperation and painstakingly accumulating and integrating insights into how a particular life has been led and lost. The process is the connection; the connection is the solace. And in this beautifully appreciative memoir, Blumberg tells us that the balm to grief is gratitude. The heart broken by loss is also sealed with gratitude, the myriad of meaningful and often happy events remembered and celebrated.

Henry Blumberg models the transformation and the importance of remembrance as essential as rites of connection. He summons the courage to read his son's papers, to ask others what they knew of him, to see his son's anguished thinking but also his acts of gentleness. He applies the same rigorous scrutiny to himself: what in his own life will give him strength, perspective, resolution and consolation.

This memoir offers a fundamental truth: that loss illuminates love's bonds, enduring and consoling.

—Jeanne Colleran, Professor Emeritus of English, John Carrol University, Ohio, United States

ACKNOWLEDGEMENTS

I am immensely grateful to all who have guided and inspired me to embark on this healing journey.

David Bergen helped me to conceive the form of my memoir and mentored me to dig down into my previously submerged feelings. The members of the Uptown Writers Group in Toronto kept me grounded as we reviewed and critiqued each other's manuscripts. David Chilton, especially, added insight.

I am extremely thankful to Dr. Jeanne Colleran for her unstinting encouragement, perceptive reading and insightful advice.

Dr. Isaac Sakinofsky read meticulously and very generously provided a range of comments that included medical aspects.

Yael Farber graciously gave permission for the title of her play, *He Left Quietly*, to be inscribed on our son's tombstone. The title of this memoir is related to those words and is so appropriate to Sean.

I greatly appreciate the support, detailed readings and constructive advice given by Dr. Frances Latchford and Dr. Kym Bird. Their input was invaluable.

I was delighted to have three family members—Jonathan Blumberg, Lisa Singer and Kate Blumberg—as readers. Their questions and suggestions were very meaningful.

Comments from other readers and interlocutors were highly valued: Stephen Barber, Anna Chatterton, Fatima Dike, Deborah Gibson, Tim Huisamen, Stephen Jennings, Ismail Mahomed, Justice Albie Sachs and Danusia Szwejkowska.

Thank you to Guy Rose of Futerman, Rose & Associates, London, for his encouragement and direction.

A special thanks to Susan Scott for her meticulous line editing of an early draft and her continuing guidance and encouragement that added immeasurably to the memoir.

I am very grateful to Ellie Barton, my editor, who provided a detailed focus on the arc of my story as well as words and nuances. Her insightful critique, laced with sensitive direction, enhanced the memoir.

Some of Sean's friends have posted regularly on Facebook to commemorate his birthday and the anniversary of his passing. These messages have been very comforting to us. Many of our friends, too numerous to mention individually, have been caring and supportive. Among those who were always there for us were Rabbi Arthur Bielfeld, Shulamith and Wilf Levin, Darren Gobert and Ross Gascho, and Carmella Veitch, and even from afar, Susan Danford, Stephen Jennings, Basil Jones and Adrian Kohler.

My beloved wife, Marcia, and I are beholden to our family for their love and unstinting care which made these times survivable. Nothing was ever too much for our children, Jonathan and Pam, Mark and Lisa, Kevin and Alisa. I want to specially mention our grandchildren, the light of our lives, whose love has sustained us: Ethan, Matthew, Theo, Kate, Mia, Evie, Julian and Bram. Our dearly beloved Sasha, who joyously grasped every moment of her two years, is forever in our hearts.

Finally, I am enormously indebted to Marcia for urging me to write this memoir. I acknowledge her ceaseless encouragement over many decades, her sensitive and attentive readings, and her advice, aware that her loving support entailed the constant revisiting of her own pain.

PROLOGUE

On August 26, 2012, our son, Sean, took his life at the age of thirty-five.

Our world changed forever.

In numb shock, we went through the arrangements between death and burial, the wrenching pain of the funeral, the seven days of shiva, the unveiling of his tombstone and the months to complete the year.

Some mourners can talk about their sorrow and in doing so achieve a measure of consolation; I was mute in my loss, my attempts to express my emotions painfully awkward. In my vulnerable state, I retreated to my study and sank into my leather chair. Behind me loomed the large mural Sean had drawn. The Ndebele motif spoke of the fight for survival against overpowering forces. In defeat, the

Ndebele people were forced to live in caves. Yet they eventually reclaimed their voices through astonishing art. I hoped that with the passage of time I too would find my own form of expression, my own voice. I had to rediscover my *Ikigai*, the purpose for my being, and to reestablish my own inner state of harmony.

It took me a long while to emerge from my inner cave. As I sat in the semi-darkness, I realized that I needed to embark on a journey of contemplation, guided by Sean's questions about family and his interest in projects and people who were striving to make the world a more just place.

I also felt acutely the need to engage with mental health issues. I recalled our helplessness as we watched Sean struggle with pain, depression and paranoia. Marcia and I often discussed whether we could have done more. As each treatment failed, we had urged him to pursue new directions.

In passing through our time of grief we realized that nothing we did, or could have done, would ultimately have made a difference.

A few friends bared their own sorrows to lessen mine. Among expressions of sympathy, I sensed the unasked question: Could it have been prevented? The pronoun *it* reflected the stigma associated with suicide. An innuendo of guilt hovered above conversations like a raven.

When a friend gave me a hug and said, "My condolences on your son's committing suicide," I cringed at the word *committing*—a word associated with crime. I thanked him for his sympathy and could say no more.

It became essential to unravel the web of shared experiences while navigating the shards of painful memories, to reach a deeper understanding of my relationship with Sean, and to rediscover what he meant to Marcia, our family and his friends. I needed, as any bereaved parent does, to find a path toward a future that provided a measure of solace. Sean often reminded Marcia and me that as the youngest of our four sons he got the least attention. Belatedly, he would now get the most.

Inspired by the memories of Sean I traversed multiple paths—indeed as if led by him. These explorations spanned continents and histories: the Holocaust in Europe, which deeply affected many generations of our family, and my four decades in apartheid South Africa, Sean's birthplace, which permeated the psyches of us all and led to our immigration to a new home in Canada.

Grief accompanied me on the journey like clouds moving slowly over the sky, sometimes obscuring the light, occasionally allowing the sun to pour through. I couldn't categorize my emotions in orderly packages, cognizant that the tide of heartache ebbs away and unexpectedly flows back.

Our initial focus was on our family and the need to come to terms with painful emotions and melancholy. Each of our sons, daughters-in-law and grandchildren have shared and created their own special memories of Sean whether through Facebook or naming a website in his honour. Whenever appropriate, our grandchildren joined us in acts of remembrance. We did not want our pain to be shrouded from any of them as a dark, unspoken family secret.

On our family odyssey we confronted, as best we could, the many obstacles: the nagging unanswered questions, the hovering shadow of guilt, the slow internal acknowledgement of his passing, the lingering sadness, knowing all the while that there can never be closure. A part of us would always dwell in the shadow cast by Sean's mental illness—an often invisible affliction found among friends, family, acquaintances and in society.

My beloved wife and I discovered solace in myriad forms in what we called our "remembrances." As if refreshing faded photographs, we uncovered recollections of joyous times, dinners, birthday celebrations, travels, shared thoughts, and especially our son's concern for family and his loving interaction with his nephews and nieces. Blended into those recollections were also meaningful religious rites, visits to his grave, and family events observing the anniversaries of his birthday and his passing.

Our remembrances did not arrive by happenstance. I mined my own memories and those of our family and pored over Sean's notebooks and drawings. I drew closer to the depth of his suffering and generosity of spirit. His friends graciously shared their memories of Sean as an exuberant teenager, before the darkness enveloped him.

In all these ways, we hold him dear. We never want him to be forgotten. We need to ensure that through our combined memories and rituals he remains an enduring beloved member of our family.

We live with the continual presence of his absence.

For our family and Sean's many friends, I have tried to capture, kindle and celebrate not only his pain but his moments of joy, his appreciation for acts of kindness, his buoyancy of spirit, especially in his teenage years, and the essence of who he was and still is to those of us who love him.

Bereavement reveals many of life's lessons. We, as so many families, have suffered the loss of parents, and, in our case, our beloved granddaughter and youngest son. And we all will experience anguish as we near the inevitable end of our own lives. I pray that our family journey will provide guideposts for you, the reader, grieving the death of a family member, a friend, a relationship or loss in any of its myriad forms.

There is no magical map through the labyrinth of mourning, but the footsteps left by those who have tread this way before signify that you are not alone. May a beacon of celebratory light guide you from the shoals of sorrow to the shores of solace.

While writing, I visualized the mythical bird, the *Sankofa*, that flies with its head turned backward. It symbolizes for the Akan people from Ghana and the Ivory Coast how the past serves as a guide for planning the future. For me, the image meant reflecting on our past to accept our future.

ONE

The Last Hug

"Please call us when you get home," I told Sean as he pulled our luggage from the trunk of our car and loaded it onto a trolley.

"I will," he promised. He understood our fears, having heard them many times.

"Sean, we want to be sure you are all right."

We weren't worried about his driving skills.

He had driven carefully on Highway 401 from our home in Toronto to the Lester B. Pearson Airport. Cars whizzed past, changing lanes. Every future drive along that road would rekindle painful memories of that day.

Sean was dressed in his usual attire, a worn grey sweatshirt. Our granddaughter, Kate, then seven, would tease her uncle about his wardrobe. "Seanie, why do you always wear grey? It's so boring."

Often to please her, he changed to a brighter colour. He loved his nephews and nieces. But when she wasn't there, he wore grey.

Marcia turned towards him. "Promise you'll call."

He nodded. We both gave him a big hug. We didn't know then the significance of that goodbye.

We watched him slowly drive away.

Sean did not call.

An hour passed. We cleared airport security. I phoned and left a message. "Please call."

Still no call. I left a message on Sean's cell phone. I tried the land line, even though he seldom answered it. In desperation, I sent a text. "Please call. If we don't hear from you, we'll ask Kevin to go and see if you're okay." Kevin, our third son, lived near Sean. I held the phone in the palm of my hand. Every few seconds I glanced at it, hoping there would be a text, or that the phone would ring, as if my staring at it would coax a response.

Two hours passed.

Still nothing.

Time to board the plane to London en route to the Edinburgh Festival.

We lined up at the gate. "Should we get on the plane or go back home?" Marcia asked. "He could have had an accident."

"He's a careful driver," I said. "I'm sure he hasn't had an accident. Maybe he went to a movie or didn't hear the phone." I was not convinced, but I felt I should say something.

We held off boarding and were among the last to take our seats.

As I lifted our luggage into the overhead bin, Marcia, in a strained voice, said, "If we haven't heard when we get to London we take the next flight back. Remember he tried twice." Then she added, "I can't forget that small scar on his neck."

After Sean's last attempt, he said he hadn't meant it seriously, that it was "a gesture." He had smiled, trying to lessen our fears, implying it was a casual signal of distress. We wanted to believe and hold onto that reassurance but dreaded the idea that he had even considered taking his own life, aware that any attempts were cries to alert us to the darkness and fears overwhelming him.

"Are you sure it's okay for us to go?" I had asked him repeatedly before we booked tickets to the Edinburgh Festival that summer.

"Things will be fine," he said. "You've been away a few times in the last year. Don't worry."

We did have a support system in place. Tuesday was his weekly appointment with his psychiatrist. Thursday was group therapy, and on Friday he saw his social worker. All of them later told Marcia and me that he had been upbeat—in retrospect a telling sign that he had made a final decision and seemed to be at peace with himself. His brothers, Jonathan, Mark and Kevin, lived nearby and would phone, visit, and invite him out. Marcia and I phoned at least twice a day, on any pretext, inquiring what mail had arrived, what he was making for supper, what arrangements he had to see his brothers. We would call to see if Sula, our small black cat, was eating her new high-protein food.

We called regularly when we travelled, whether in Canada, Europe, India or South Africa.

And yet, despite everything, there was only so much we could do.

"If he wants to do it, he will," Sean's psychiatrist had told us many times. "And there is nothing you can do about it." That was the line we repeated to ourselves. Still, it was so hard to believe it.

Two years earlier, we were waiting for Sean to arrive at Kevin and Alisa's house for the family seder. I called him repeatedly. No response. Eventually, we sat down to the ritual meal. As we were approaching the stage where the youngest child asks, "*Ma Nishtana*" (Why is this night different from all other nights?), my cell phone rang. We were about to find out how different this night would be.

"I'm at Sherbourne Street where it passes over Rosedale Valley Road," Sean said softly.

I knew what that meant. From the overpass, he could jump into the stream of cars below. "We have to leave. Sorry. It's urgent," I said. I whispered to Marcia what he had said. We rushed out without explaining—there was no point in the whole family hastening to Sean.

I drove as fast as I could from Downsview to Sherbourne Street in the height of evening traffic, weaving among the honking cars. I was oblivious to speed limits, desperate to get to the overpass in time.

I parked near the bridge and we started walking.

"There he is," Marcia pointed. "I'll go on my own. You stay here. If we both rush up to him, he might jump."

Marcia knew more of Sean's fears than I. She had spent the past year talking with him daily, for hours at a time. All this, during her sabbatical from York University.

I watched in a stupor as she walked towards our son, aware that each step was fraught with danger. I saw them talking at the parapet. I prayed that she could coax him away, terrified that with a sudden lunge he would hurl himself onto the streaming cars below.

At times my breathing stopped. I imagined Marcia's dread, and Sean's fears—whatever drew him to the edge. One wrong word could have disastrous consequences.

I lost all track of time until at long last he slowly moved away from the wall. When he and Marcia joined me, I tried to appear calm and speak softly, despite my inner agitation. I stopped myself from suggesting that we go to North York General Hospital where he had been a patient, or contact his psychiatrist, afraid that he'd turn angry and rush back to the overpass. "Sean, I'm relieved you're okay. Let's talk about it," I said.

"Where?" he asked. He looked unsure of what to do.

"There's a coffee shop down the road."

As we sat and talked, Marcia's paper cup shook slightly every time she lifted it to take a sip.

"Sean," I reassured him, "we know things are upsetting you. Please tell us."

He did not reply.

We repeated what we had said many times before, that we

would do whatever possible to help him. We didn't know what else to say. I wanted to engage him in conversation, hoping to lessen his anxiety. He kept staring at the table top, saying he was fine. After a while he looked up.

"It's the condo," he said. "Someone's trying to steal it from me."

Marcia and I had helped Sean purchase a condo on Sheppard Avenue.

"How?" I asked.

"By forging my signature."

"Sean, as a lawyer, I promise you that won't happen."

His eyes fixed on me. "And if it does, what will you do?"

Calmly, I explained that forgery was out of the question. After a while he looked up at me and gave a faint smile. I was relieved. In helping him confront his anxieties and paranoia, I hoped reason would prevail, even as I realized his anxiety could overrule all rationality.

He asked me to provide reassurance in writing.

I wrote a note on a scrap of paper saying that I would ensure he wouldn't lose his condo. I hoped that would satisfy him. I wanted him to know he had nothing to fear. Fortunately, that was enough to persuade him to come home with us.

These were my thoughts as the plane taxied prior to takeoff, not knowing what we were leaving behind, fearful of what we would learn when we landed in London.

Marcia gripped my hand. "Maybe we shouldn't have left."

"We've been away many times. Everything was fine. Things will be okay."

"We've done everything possible. I hope it's enough," she whispered.

There wasn't much to say, and the supper tasted like cardboard.

The overnight flight felt interminable. My chest tightened from time to time in the darkened cabin. "I'm sure he's fine," I kept saying. I didn't know. Maybe repeating it as a mantra would make it so.

As I shifted in my seat, I felt the small key ring in my pocket shaped like an inukshuk, an Inuit talisman. I carried it with me hoping that it would provide direction or warn of impending danger. Touching it gave me a measure of comfort for the road ahead.

In my jumbled thoughts, I kept questioning why Sean did not answer the phone. While fearing the worst, my mind flitted to another scene. When I was eight years old, I watched my dad, Julius, listening to the news on the crackling radio in our sitting room. This was in South Africa during the dark days of World War II. "I wonder if any family in Libau survived," he said. It was a phrase he would repeat to me every few days. Now I understand his fear for the lives of his parents, brothers, sister and cousins. Not only was he powerless to help them, he did not even know if they were alive or dead.

Dad, when he was ten years old, was sent by his parents, Jacob and Ernestine, from the port of Libau, in Latvia, to the United States. I once asked him why his parents did that. The idea of leaving my family at such an age frightened me. "I left with an aunt who needed medical attention in America," he said. As simple as that. No more explanation.

I imagined him as a small boy in short trousers, dwarfed among the masses of emigrants travelling steerage, pressing to board. Walking up the gangplank, he clutched his tiny case. What could he possibly take with him? Clothing, bread, cheese, a few toys? Perhaps mounting the steps of an ocean liner bound for New York seemed like a great adventure. He could not then have known that he would never again see his family, nor his old hometown of Libau.

When he first told me of leaving his parents, I was too young to appreciate the significance of this wrenching departure. I simply hoped that such separation would never happen to me.

Right up to his death in 1963, he searched for family, hoping to discover that someone had survived. He did not find a soul. Many years later I learned that Dad's parents, his brothers Jossel and Leopold, and his sister, Fannie, had all been murdered. Dad was the sole surviving descendant. It was a blessing, I believe, that he was spared the devastating truth. And yet throughout his life, Dad carried the pain of this separation, never seeing his parents or family again.

I visualized my grandparents on the wharf, hugging their small son goodbye, choking back tears as the steamship pulled out of the harbour. Now, a father and grandfather myself, I could relate to their fear of never seeing him again, questioning whether they had made the right decision. I imagined their frantic concern until that first letter from New York, saying he'd arrived safely. I knew exactly what it would mean for them to wait anxiously, all their lives, for each scrap of news about their son.

As I think of my grandparents, waving at their son growing smaller and smaller until he became a blur, I see Sean pulling away from the curb at the airport, the car merging with the flow of traffic, disappearing out of sight.

"If we don't hear from Sean now," Marcia repeated as the plane descended at Heathrow, "we take the next flight home."

The plane hit the tarmac. I checked my text messages to see one from Kevin. "Sean's fine."

My phone rang as I pulled our carry-on luggage from the overhead bin. Kevin had tracked the flight. "He's fine," Kevin said. "He called me after your plane left. He said he got your messages but fell asleep and didn't hear the ringing."

I was skeptical that Sean hadn't heard the many calls. Two phones had been ringing, the land line and his cell with its incessant beeps.

It was early in the morning, London time. He was fine. He would probably be asleep now. I called him later.

"Sorry about that," he said. "I was asleep and didn't hear the phone. Maybe my cell was in another room."

"When we get to Edinburgh we'll call to say hello. Please answer your phone," I said.

He promised that he would and wished us a safe trip.

"It's all strange. I hope he's okay," I said, looking at Marcia.

"You know if anything happens to him, our lives will never be the same," she said. She was right. Thank God he was alive and fine, for now.

After a week at the Edinburgh Festival, we were heading home. I had spoken to Sean the afternoon before. He sounded subdued. We called him again early in the morning, while packing to leave. It was nearly midnight in Toronto, a time when he would usually be awake. When I got his voicemail, I left a message for him to call us. Instinctively, I also sent a text. Every time we had called him during the previous week, he had answered his phone.

We boarded the plane for London on our way home to Toronto without having had any contact with Sean. We had checked into the Air Canada lounge in Heathrow Airport on the stopover only to learn that our plane would be delayed four hours. If all went well, we would be home by 1 a.m. I had called his cell phone and left messages saying that the plane was late. I asked him to call back. I followed up with a text message. To Marcia I said, "It's not good that he's not answering."

An hour passed. No response. Again, I called and texted.

After three hours I again called his cell phone and land line, leaving a message on voicemail. "If you don't call back," I said, "we'll ask Kevin to go over and check if you're okay." I followed up with a text message and an email. Again, no response. Marcia suggested we call Kevin. "Why bug Kevin?" I said. "Sean's probably fine, like the last time."

She pleaded for me to call. I knew she couldn't.

"He probably fell asleep," Kevin said.

"Tell him it's important," Marcia urged. "I want him to go and check on Sean."

Kevin offered to drive by Sean's with Alisa and the kids.

We watched the departure board, waiting for Kevin's call, then lingered at the back of the line as the time came to board the plane. We checked in at the gate. Suddenly, as we neared the door of the plane, my phone rang. It was Kevin. His voice was barely audible.

"Sean committed suicide."

"What do you mean?" It couldn't be true.

"He committed suicide. I found him," Kevin repeated.

"Are you sure?"

"Yes, I'm sure."

"Is he dead?" I asked, as if in a trance.

"Yes."

Marcia stood next to me, watching. There was nothing I could say to soften the blow.

"That was Kevin. Sean is dead," I whispered.

"Oh my God." She stared at me, stunned, her face drained of all colour.

"Please stay here." I retraced my steps to the gate to speak with the attendant. If we upgraded to business class, we would have more privacy on the agonizing flight home.

"Is it possible to get—buy—two upgrades to business class?"

The attendant looked up at me in surprise.

"We've just heard our son took his own life."

"Sorry, we're full," she snapped and walked away. I had the feeling she was thinking, *My God what people will do to get an upgrade.*

Waiting for takeoff, I stared at the grey seat in front of me. The tubular-shaped interior closed in on me, the air stifling. I became aware of each breath passing through my nostrils, scratching my dry throat. *Why?* Why did Sean end his life? I thought of the deep wounds that punctured him, wounds that I had tried to understand but never fully fathomed.

Marcia and I had feared this day would come, yet when it did, it was impossible to believe the worst had actually happened. I struggled to reconcile the distance between desperately hoping his death hadn't happened and being forced to accept that it had. I agonized over the unexpectedness, the uncontrollability, the finality of his death.

"There are things we have to do," I said. Doing anything was better than staring at the seat in front of me, asking questions with no answers, waiting for takeoff. I shifted into pragmatic mode and phoned Jonathan and Mark, leaving urgent messages for them to call Kevin.

I called our rabbi. He had retired ten years earlier, but we continued to think of him as our rabbi. From the time we arrived in Canada in 1980, Rabbi Bielfeld had celebrated all our happy events and grieved with us when we mourned the loss of family.

"Rabbi, Sean has taken his life. Will you officiate at the funeral?" I asked.

"That's terrible. Of course I will." Then he added softly, "He was such a lovely guy."

We called Sean's psychiatrist. He had seen Sean that week. He sounded devastated. I sensed he would be shaken by those haunting questions: Could he have done more? Did we blame him in some way?

"We want to thank you for all you did," I said. "You gave Sean two more years."

His voice choked with emotion as he thanked me. We both knew that Sean had endured physical pain, depression and paranoia for many years.

As the plane became airborne, Marcia reminded me of her many talks with our dear friend Stephen about suicide by friends of his who were living with AIDS. Stephen had emphasized their strength and courage, and in her shocked state Marcia remembered those words. Sean's situation, though, was different. He had fought for nearly fifteen years in the darkness of depression and distress of paranoia. "We must respect Sean's decision," she said. She looked directly at me. "Our lives will never be the same. It's going to be tough for both of us, for everyone in our family, for friends and all those who knew Sean and loved him."

The anguish of our loss would either fray or strengthen the bonds of love that had sustained us for forty-six years.

"I have a feeling that Sean had already decided before we left,"

Marcia said. "Maybe that's why he didn't answer the phone when we called from the Toronto airport. He had already said his final goodbye."

I held her hand tight.

At last, the plane taxied into Lester B. Pearson Airport. "I wonder if anyone will be here to meet us," Marcia said.

"Maybe they'll be at the house," I said, trying to forestall any disappointment.

It was nearly two in the morning when we finally pushed our baggage trolley into the concourse. There were Jonathan, Mark and Kevin, together, near the entrance. We were so relieved, and yet their sheer presence underscored the absence of our fourth son. In our shocked state, there wasn't much to say. All we could do was hug each other. Family togetherness meant more now than ever before.

Soon enough, we heard the story—how Kevin went to check on Sean while Alisa and their three children, Matthew, Kate and Julian, stayed in the car. Kevin dragged out each sentence as he drove us home. He had found Sean slumped with a helium mask covering his face. This would have been the most painless way to die. Kevin called Alisa from the car to join him, then phoned 911.

I believed that the shock of finding Sean as they did would sear their psyches. That pain would gnaw at them for the rest of their lives.

Kevin had rushed back to the car to tell the children to stay put. "You stay here, in the car. Don't come out."

Matthew, Kate and Julian would have watched the unfolding drama. Police arriving, sirens blaring. Fire engine and ambulance, lights flashing. Paramedics and police, running. The children were unaware of what was really happening. Kevin would later explain to them as gently as possible that Sean had passed away.

Kevin had also called Jonathan and Mark. Jonathan rushed over. Mark, Lisa and their sons, Ethan and Theo, had arrived at our family cottage in Muskoka a few hours before Kevin's call. They repacked immediately and drove the two-and-a-half hours back to Toronto.

It was nearly 3 a.m. when we arrived home to find our friends,

Shulamith and Wilf, standing in the dark driveway. They had been close family friends since before Sean was born and were particularly attached to him. As we got out of the car, they embraced us. Kevin had called them.

"You both did everything you could. You couldn't have done more," Shulamith said as she hugged Marcia.

We would never forget their kindness in waiting for us, nor the comfort of their words.

The next day on the seat of Marcia's Acura I found a crumpled gas receipt from the Esso service station on Lawrence Avenue. I wondered, Was Sean leaving a message?

800 LAWRENCE AVENUE
NORTH YORK, ON M3C
URN:R121461107
08/26/2012 768112055
01:36:09 AM

PUMP
SUPR 38.635L
PRICE/L 1.449
FUEL TOTAL $ 55.98

HST in fuel $ 6.44
INTERAC $ 55.98

TYPE: PURCHASE
ACCOUNT: CHEQUING $55.98
CARD NUMBER: C ************4901
DATE/TIME: 2012/08/26 01:36:06
A- INTERAC
LOYALTY: NO

SEE OVER. VOIR AU VERSO. SEE OVER. VOIR

Later, at the condo, Kevin pointed to Sean's computer. Next to it was a sheet of paper listing all his passwords. Neatly stacked in rows were bottles of meds and a small stack of cards: his Visa, library card, driver's licence, health card.

I asked Kevin about the contents of a brown folder, filled with papers.

"That's his computer printout of the way he took his life. He got it from the internet," Kevin said.

"Why would he leave a printout?"

"To make sure no one could be accused of assisting in his suicide."

I took the gas receipt from my pocket and carefully pressed out the creases.

Kevin watched me. "Sean filled Mom's car. It was his last purchase."

Sean preferred to drive Marcia's Acura when we were away. The deal was that we filled the car with gas when we left and he filled it before our return. He had kept his side of the bargain. He had left that receipt to show he hadn't forgotten to fill up the car, as promised.

I read the time-stamp: 1:30 a.m. the previous morning.

I stared at the time, understanding its significance.

Filling the car was part of his saying goodbye. Even in his most desperate moment, he had not acted impulsively. Perhaps he had even chosen to end his life just before we were scheduled to fly home from Edinburgh, to save our returning early.

I stared, fixated, at the little gas receipt between my fingers. I could barely read the words and letters. Eventually, I placed the receipt in a plastic container.

In the coming weeks, I would use this container to collect his diary, notebooks, letters, paintings, books, poems and art. I collected but did not look. I was fearful of what I might discover.

One day, I would have to face its contents. How would I know when I was ready?

TWO

To Keep Walking

In the hours that immediately followed, I flitted between different states of mind, facing the painful realities of the many decisions to be made: choosing a casket at Benjamin's Park Memorial Chapel, composing death notices for the newspapers and the internet, lining up the pallbearers, arranging for the limousine, contacting people about the funeral. These ritualized decisions, for the moment, shrouded death's finality.

There was another issue to attend to, but we did not know how.

Sean had often spoken of his "friend" but never mentioned her by name. All we knew was that they went to movies or out for lunch together, and that he had bought her a puppy. Now we had to decide whether to contact her, assuming we could even find her.

Surely she had known his intentions. He had planned each step carefully. And yet if he had told her, or hinted at his plans, she would have tried desperately to dissuade him and sought help to restrain him.

We decided she should be told. If she simply called his cell phone, we would know how to connect with her.

A day went by without a call. Kevin opened Sean's phone. Tellingly, though a very private person, he had left his phone unlocked. We watched anxiously as Kevin scrolled through Sean's contacts, calls received and sent, text messages and emails.

"Maybe Sean unlocked his phone hoping we would trace her," I said.

Marcia nodded while watching Kevin closely. After a while, Kevin found the number.

I dreaded calling her. How do you tell someone their friend just took his life?

The phone rang for a while before a woman answered, softly. "Yes."

"Are you Sean's friend?" I asked.

Silence. She must have wondered who I was and why I was calling.

"I think so."

"I'm Sean's father. I am so sorry to tell you—" I choked up. "Sean passed away yesterday."

"What are you saying?" There was utter disbelief in her voice. I gently repeated the message in different words. It was clear to me they were more than "just friends."

We would never know why Sean hadn't introduced us or told us her name. I imagine he would have been happy to know we had reached out to Suja.

"Do you want to see Sean before the interment?" the undertaker asked.

I hesitated. Did I want my last sight of Sean to be of him smiling and hugging us goodbye at the airport or lying on a gurney? I wanted to remember both.

The undertaker led us to a room. Sean was lying on a table, cloaked in a white shroud.

A guardian—a *shomer*, an elderly, white-bearded man in skullcap and prayer shawl—sat a few feet away. The guardian's role was to watch over Sean from the time the coroner released the body to the funeral home until burial. In Jewish tradition the dead should not be abandoned prior to arriving in their new earthly home, as the soul hovers over the body in limbo until it is interred. The *shomer* seemed oblivious to our entering the room. His lips moved while he read Hebrew psalms and watched over Sean's body, comforting his spirit in its state of transition.

Sean lay outstretched as if in a deep, peaceful slumber. My eyes dimmed as I felt the intensity of his spirit bathing and enveloping his body.

I gently rubbed his white, soft shoulder. "Seanie wake up. Wake up," I whispered. I knew deep inside me that he couldn't wake, but I desperately hoped that he would. I simply had to try.

Upon our return home, we found a chicken potpie wedged between two bags of ice on Sean's chair on our front porch, with a card from our friends Darren and Ross expressing their heartfelt condolences. Sean often sat in that chair to enjoy the afternoon sun. I later asked Darren where they got the ice. He laughed. "We wanted to leave something for you knowing how painful your visit to the undertakers would be. When we arrived at your house, nobody was home. We couldn't just leave the pie to bake in the hot sun. So we went to Longo's supermarket down the road and bought ice."

As I reflect on the anguish of that day, this act of spontaneous, heartwarming kindness is especially treasured among the many other acts of caring that we value.

Sean would have been amazed at the hundreds of people at Temple Emanu-El in Toronto on the morning of August 30, 2012, at his service. So many people crowded into the sanctuary that the caretaker had to bring in extra rows of chairs. If we could have told

Sean, he would have grinned and said, "There must have been another event on the go. It couldn't be for me."

Marcia and I took our place in the front row, near the casket. I put my arm around her. "It feels so strange. He was only thirty-five. So much younger than us, yet there in the coffin," I said. Marcia nodded. My throat tightened.

As I stared at the pine coffin, I imagined Sean in the stillness of the night, preparing to take his life. I was reminded of the Aokigahara Forest, known as the Forest of Tears, on the flank of Mount Fuji. Many die there by suicide each year. It is a place where, according to anthropologist Karen Nakamura, "You won't die alone." A shiver surged through me as I imagined my son sitting alone, taking his life.

In front of him sat two dolls to keep him company, so he would not be on his own. One a small, cute teddy bear in a red cardigan and checked jacket—a gift from Danusia, Sean's former fiancée. Next to the bear sat a doll with white hair and a warm smile who represented Sean's hero, Nelson Mandela, affectionately known by his Xhosa clan name, Madiba. We had bought that doll when Marcia, Sean and I, along with Danusia, visited South Africa five years before. The iconic shirt symbolized to me Madiba's expression of relief from the restraints of his imprisonment. For Sean, the doll could have signified a release from his own inner captivity.

The small companions sat in front of him as he took his last breath—the one a symbol of bravery and courage, the other of love. They would have been the last objects he saw as his eyes closed. Perhaps they gave him comfort on the next stage of his journey.

We have kept the dolls together ever since.

At the service, one person from each of the three generations in our family offered a eulogy.

Marcia went first. She walked slowly to the podium and steadied herself as she nearly tripped on the stairs. A few days before, she had said to me, "I will speak. I know you won't be able to." Despite being numb with shock, Marcia summoned the strength for this caring act to honour her son. As I listened, I was struck by the irony of my silence—a lawyer and the designated speaker at family events who could not bring himself to speak. I would have lost my composure.

Marcia addressed Sean:

We are heartbroken as a family and feel your loss acutely. At the same time, we respect your decision and know you are now, at last, at peace. This is a comfort to us and we will always lovingly hold you in our hearts and minds. Your decision was made after much thought and suffering, and all we as a family can now do is to keep your memory alive. That doesn't mean the heartbreak doesn't remain.

Our eldest grandchild, eleven-year-old Ethan, then walked up to the podium. He seemed so small.

"He's got amazing courage. More than I have today," I whispered to Marcia as I squeezed her hand.

"Sean was a caring uncle," Ethan said. "He liked to talk to me about hockey, which was good because my mom and dad don't know anything about hockey. He enjoyed coming to my hockey games and was my biggest fan."

Ethan stopped speaking for a few moments as if unable to continue. My heart sank. Then he smiled at the hundreds of mourners sitting before him. "We went on a family cruise. Seanie and I watched movies late at night after my mom and dad were asleep, and we ate lots of ice cream because it was free." I heard quiet laughter.

Jonathan, Sean's oldest brother, rose and spoke next.

Brother, you burned so brightly, were wise and sensitive beyond your years. As the youngest of us four, you were so expert at being heard. When a teenager you painted all over the walls of your room and so you painted a bright swatch around the lives of your friends. You were the sportiest Blumberg. A contrarian. Alternatively intense and lighthearted.

Jonathan read a message from a friend of Sean: "Sean, you remain forever in my mind as the most vibrant, exciting, and imaginative boyhood friend I had. There was the wonderful canoe trip we took at Killarney and the picture of a chipmunk eating an apple out of your hand—your gentleness was palpable."

My mind flitted to a time when Sean and I were canoeing in Killarney Provincial Park on Georgian Bay. The water turned choppy in the rising wind that pushed us farther from shore. Dark, swirling clouds warned of an impending storm.

"We have to get to shore quickly," Sean shouted above the wind. He started paddling furiously.

"Paddle slower!" I yelled. "We're going to capsize."

"Don't worry," he shouted.

Somehow, he got us to the shore. The wind subsided and the clouds departed as quickly as they had come. We hauled the canoe onto the grassy bank and basked in the sun. We had survived.

I looked at the plain pine casket in the Temple sanctuary and closed my eyes for a moment as the tears spilled out.

I imagined Sean crossing the river Styx in a rowboat with his sole companion Charon, the Greek mythological ferryman, who carried the souls of the newly deceased across the boundary between earth and the netherworld. I feared for his uncertain journey. Yet I was comforted, believing Sean would reach the Elysian Fields, the final resting place of virtuous souls. He had lived a life filled with care and compassion, despite his own deep pain.

As I thought of Sean's passage, I also feared for the uncertain journey that Marcia and I, indeed our whole family, were now making. What shore would we reach?

Listening to Jonathan at the podium, I wished we had taken more canoe trips and that I had spent more time with our four sons when they were growing up. It had been a tough balancing act: time with family, building a law practice in South Africa, immigrating to Canada, requalifying and opening my own law firm in Toronto.

My thoughts drifted to my first canoe trip with Jonathan, in Algonquin Park. After we had paddled for a few hours and eased our canoe onto a small sandbank, Jonathan said, “We have to do a portage here somewhere.” We pushed our way through the bushes, shouldering the canoe and supplies. There was no sign of a trail. “I’m not sure if we’re going in the right direction,” Jonathan said. “Stay here and I’ll go look. I won’t be long.” He disappeared into the forest.

I waited, expecting he would soon return. Mosquitos swarmed my hands, face and legs. I slapped at them, many bloated with my blood. I glanced at my watch. Maybe Jonathan was lost. I vacillated between wanting to search for him, get help, or stay put. Each alternative had its dangers. If I remained, at least he would know where to find me. My indecision heightened. A chilling emptiness grew in my chest. What if we were both lost?

Eventually I heard a crashing sound in the bush. Jonathan appeared, saying excitedly, “I found the way. It’s near.”

“What took you so long?”

“I got lost.”

That wasn’t the answer I wanted to hear.

As the service continued, I snapped out of the reverie, feeling light-headed. I feared I myself was lost, floating in the middle of a large, unknown lake in a paddle-less canoe.

Our sons, their spouses and children travelled in one limousine to the Pardes Shalom Cemetery. In another accompanying us was Solly, a close friend from Philadelphia, and Marcia’s cousin, Anthony, from New York. Marcia whispered to me, “It was wonderful of them to drop everything to be with us.”

Suja, her eyes red and tear-stained, also rode with us. Her daughter accompanied her for support.

Bereavement bonded us all.

As if in a stupor, I watched our traditional burial process: the coffin borne by the pallbearers, Rabbi Bielfeld intoning blessings, the cantor chanting, the casket slowly being lowered into the freshly dug, gaping hole. At the end, mourners came forward and took turns shovelling clods of earth into the grave. With each thump on the lid of the coffin I felt a stabbing pain, knowing that our beloved, gentle Sean was inside.

We entered the mourning period called *shiva*. For seven days our family gathered to receive visitors, participate in prayers and express condolences. Some sent donations to a fund in Sean's memory or brought meals to the house.

The support of our sons, daughters-in-law and grandchildren helped us survive. All had to deal with their own intense suffering, yet were eager to ease Marcia's and my pain, and in so doing helped unite the family in consolation.

Friends and extended family connected with us to share our grief. Sometimes only a few words were exchanged with a firm handshake or a meaningful hug, filled with feeling and expressions of sympathy.

Our dear friend Stephen wrote about the family, in particular Sean: "It's hard to say which aspects of Sean's friendship are farthest beyond price. No happiness was more uplifting than his, no principled life more instructive, no kindness more penetrating."

We appreciated a thoughtful post on Facebook by Sean's friend, Lucky Budd:

For those of us who can't be at Sean's funeral at noon tomorrow, I am suggesting we take a time out to observe a moment of silence to support the Blumberg family.

Sean taught all of us a ton about compassion, love and giving. It is my honour to take a moment in solidarity with you all and those in Toronto to give thanks to my old friend, and feel thankful that he is finally at peace.

Some mourners shared with us the lingering hurt they seldom bared to others: their struggle to deal with a family member's mental illness, the estrangement of a son or daughter, the unexpected death of a child, a parent, a close relative. People opened up, hoping that their sharing would, in some way, alleviate our grief. One friend told me his daughter had not spoken to him for five years. He did not know where she was or how to contact her. The tears in his eyes spoke of his anguish. My cousin Brian in Johannesburg called and confided that when he was a teenager, he had tried to take his own life in a shed in the garden. Fortunately, the gardener found him and rushed him to the hospital. He was fortunate, he said, to be saved in time.

Another friend sat down next to me. His son, who was living in Asia, had phoned a month before to say it would be his last call home. As my friend spoke, his eyes filled with the pain of that gut-wrenching call. He smiled as he added how relieved he and his wife were when their son called the next morning and apologized, saying he was now in a different space. He feared another similar phone call.

People could bare their wounds, knowing we would understand. I could only nod, agree and thank them as I felt a strange urge to console them.

The evening before the funeral there had been a ring at our front door.

Marcia asked, "Who could that be?"

"No idea who'd come around at this hour." I opened the door to Andre, a client. He apologized for coming late at night and gave me a hug. Andre had come to Canada as a young man after having served in the French Foreign Legion. Like us, he had planted new family roots in Canada. "I would like to come to the funeral, but I can't," he said as I led him into the family room.

He looked down at the carpet for a few moments as if trying to compose himself. "My father took his own life when I was only sixteen years old. I found him. He hanged himself. I cut the rope around his neck and tried to revive him but he was already dead. I've never gotten over what happened."

He did not have to say more; he understood our pain. I had never suspected that beneath the tough demeanour of this former soldier lay his own inescapable agony.

"It must have opened a deep wound for him to visit us the night before the funeral," I said to Marcia after he had left.

The last image of a tormented father continued to haunt the son, who reached out to us in empathy.

One afternoon a friend came to offer his condolences. This was a man with three children, each exceptionally talented and intelligent. Tragically, two of them had taken their own lives. As he walked in, he came straight to me and gave me a lengthy hug.

"I know," he said.

I knew that he knew. He didn't have to say anything more; there was nothing more to say. We spoke of life and death. He reminisced about the recent passing of his mother.

"Part of her philosophy was to always be prepared," he said. "She was fully prepared."

I later found that applied to Sean as well; he had meticulously planned and executed each step once he decided to take his life.

"It's difficult when there's a change of the natural order," my friend observed. "When an aged parent dies there is great mourning, but everyone knows that it follows the expected rhythm of life, which not even the most powerful rulers and dictators can change. But when a child or grandchild dies, there's a different kind of grief—and lingering questions of whether we could have done more. Some will continue to question why it happened. Others pray the person will be at rest, understanding the depth of suffering."

As he spoke, I remembered that Sean's decision had been made after years of emotional and physical anguish, in addition to all that careful thought.

"You know the story of Daedelus and Icarus," he continued. "Icarus soared high before the fall. A lot has been written about that fable, but who else suffered other than Icarus?"

I couldn't answer.

"His father, Daedelus, made the wings that allowed his son to soar. Then his son died."

Marcia and I had made Sean's wings. We watched him soar into the brilliant light of the sun and then descend into a darkness from which no one could wrest him free.

I walked my friend to the door. He grasped my hand and came close. "I can't forget," he said, "after the funeral of my second child, you asked how I could continue walking. At times I myself wondered, but I forced myself to do so."

I nodded, surprised that many years later, he recalled my words.

Our family, and Sean's close friends, would have to discover how to deal with every painful step.

The week of mourning ended; all who had come to condole on the last night of shiva had left. During the week the house had been packed. Memories had been exchanged, grief shared. Now it was palpably quiet. Marcia and I slumped in the family room, facing an emptiness that cried out to be filled.

THREE

The Storm

I will never forget the wild storm a few weeks after Sean's funeral.

Late one afternoon the sky darkened, and lightning flashed to the clap of thunder. The wind whistled and howled around the house. The rain started as a drizzle then burst into sheets of water that beat down on the roof and windows. Our three sons and their wives were sitting in the family room. Some of our grandchildren were chasing each other excitedly in variations of hide and seek, while others were busy in the basement with Lego, train engines, carriages and rails, all kept for the best of times.

Lisa, Mark's wife, went downstairs to check on the kids. "There's water damage down here," she called. We rushed to the basement and inspected every room. Strangely, only Sean's room, where had lived before moving to his apartment, was wet. The possessions he had left behind were still in that room. My shoes squeaked on the waterlogged carpet.

The bed, desk and bookcase all looked fine. I ran my hands along the base of the furniture; the wood was spongy and saturated. Thankfully, Sean's books and papers were dry. I opened the filing cabinet; the files were undamaged. Only the carpet and furniture were ruined.

This was the first major flood damage in the thirty years we had lived in our Toronto home. Previously, there had been only two or three minor roof leaks. I went through the house, relieved to see there was no other damage, yet dejected that Sean's old room had flooded. "Sean," I said, "is telling us he wants us to move on."

Marcia looked at me and nodded.

It was time to deal with his possessions, something we had been unable to face.

Disposing of a loved one's belongings deepens the grief.

The soggy carpet and damaged furniture were easy to discard. Katie helped us pack the clothing he left into plastic bags for charities. She held up his drab grey sweatshirt and asked if she could take it. She reminded us how he used to laugh whenever she asked him if he didn't have anything else to wear. We were happy to give it to her. I pulled the coloured folders from the filing cabinet and placed them in plastic boxes. Those folders contained his notes of visits to psychiatrists, therapists, doctors, copies of medical prescriptions, notes about meditation and yoga classes—a chronicle of his last fifteen years. Then there were his old bank and credit card statements—the easiest for me to shred. After that, I couldn't throw out anything else. I knew I would have to go through each item, apprehensive of what I might discover. In my excessive need to preserve everything, I even kept staplers, stationery, soft toys and ballpoint pens.

I glanced at the headings of the files I'd removed from the filing cabinet to try and understand, again, the demons that had stalked him, and to begin to fathom his struggle to explore every avenue until he faced a stone wall that led him to plan his leaving. I pulled out a thin brown folder. On its tab he'd scrawled, *God I Hope This Pain Will Go Away.* The pain never did go away. I put the file back. I wasn't ready to face its contents.

As I did this, I felt him near me. I wanted Sean to believe we tried to comprehend his pain while we recognized the chasm between knowing and feeling. I longed to tell him how much we missed him, but realized for the umpteenth time that was simply impossible. I continued sorting the files, glancing at the headings, and as I did, my fingers froze. I was unable to turn the pages. When would I find the courage to delve in, in earnest? In truth, I was uncertain that that time would ever come.

Then I found the plastic bins, three in all. I pried open the lid of the first one to find five photograph albums. I turned the plastic sleeves. Sean had carefully sorted memories of friends and family. There were photos of Marcia, Sean and me, as well as of adored nephews and nieces dating back to their gurgling infancy. There were photos of his brothers in bar-mitzvah suits with shirts, ties and neatly combed hair, as well as snapshots of them casually dressed at family gatherings. I lingered over pictures of his school friends and companions, portrayed in goofy poses at parties and on travels to Europe and Israel. All reflected moments of joy: the warmth of loving family relationships and friendships.

The next plastic container held books, medical records, magazines and music tapes. Scattered among them were birthday cards from family. There were printed and hand-drawn cards, lovingly inscribed, from adoring school and university friends, all from a time before the darkness set in.

The third box was filled with his drawings, small and large black notebooks, and a blue book embossed in gold letters with the word "Diary." I dreaded opening it. This would be the hardest box to deal with. I was overwhelmed by the daunting task of entering the world of his most intimate thoughts and pain. I picked up the diary and held it for a few moments, unable to open it. I put it back. I felt like an intruder in his private space.

A few months later when I summoned the courage and anxiously opened his diary, I saw that it only related to his late teens and early twenties. My tension eased; this was a time too early to give any insight into his final actions.

I scanned the pages at random and stumbled on an entry about the 1989 Academy Award-winning film, *My Left Foot*, Irishman Christy Brown's autobiography. Born with cerebral palsy, Christy learns to paint and write with only the toes of his left foot. While some people, at the time, considered him "retarded," Christy's mother never gave up on him. He became a novelist, painter and poet. I understood this choice of film. Sean, in his own struggle, had sought inspiration from the courage and determination of Christy Brown. I thought of the years of art therapy, cognitive behavioural therapy, counselling; appointments with psychiatrists, physiotherapists, doctors; mornings of meditation and yoga. Sean tried everything to fight depression and physical pain, to confront the anxiety and paranoid fears. I hoped he also believed that Marcia and I would never give up on him. As I read, the page blurred. Again, my fingers froze.

I stared at the containers on the floor beside me filled with details of his life and dreams, his hopes, loves, pain, and his struggle against darkness. I was driven to understand more about him—what he had endured and the impact he had made on the lives of our family and friends. I knew that much would be unfathomable; still, that he had meticulously filed his papers signified to me that he wanted to preserve a record of his life. It was as if he expected someone to go through all this material carefully, after he was gone.

He was right.

We found no suicide note from Sean. Instead, he had prepared everything, to a minute degree. A note would have been superfluous.

On the top shelf of Sean's bookcase I found a Plaster of Paris recreation of a Norman stone sculpture. As I examined the warrior, I wondered about the artist.

I turned over the piece to read that Sean had made it as a school project in 1992. Barely sixteen at the time, he had written this inscription: "Norman Stone Sculpture original made in 1067 recreated by the Canadian artist Sean Blumberg. Produced and ideas by Sean Blumberg. Special thanks to The Blumberg Family for their unending support." I was moved by this expression of thankfulness to the family. Later, I discovered that his appreciation went far deeper than I could have imagined. His impish humour surfaced in the scrawl, "and to the Norman warriors who modelled for the sculpture."

I suppose I had seen this piece in 1992, but seeing it again I marvelled at his talent, depicting a battle-ready knight in armour with shield, poised to strike at his enemy. In retrospect, the knight epitomized the bravery and courage the young Sean would need for his own struggles. The Normans, in their conquest of England, were aliens; I imagine that their sense of being outsiders must have resonated with him. The shield was adorned with a large crucifix, emphasizing the religious zeal that emboldened the warrior in the face of his adversaries. I couldn't help but think that such determination spoke to Sean's fervour to conquer his own fears.

On the side of the warrior's head, under his helmet, was a ghost motif—a spectral figure that I assumed Sean had drawn to represent himself.

Even at age sixteen, I believe, Sean was envisioning himself boldly doing battle—not with an outside enemy, but with his own internal demons.

A few days later, emotionally drained, I stopped sorting his papers for a time and sat in my study, in my swivel chair, hoping to focus

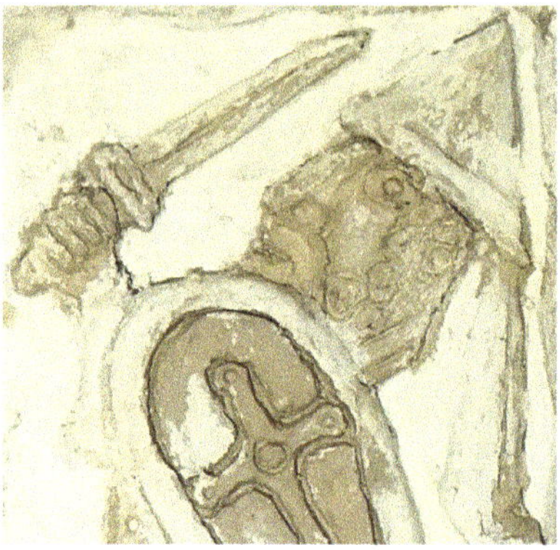

on something that would let my mind wander for a spell. I stared at the mural on the wall behind me, and found myself transfixed by its distinctive geometric shapes: the red centre surrounded by green; the black-and-white borders; the bold blue and ochre colours. When Sean was about sixteen, he'd asked if he could paint a mural in the Ndebele tradition in my study. When the mural was completed, I was surprised by the size—it covered most of the wall.

At the time, I thought of the mural as a powerful symbolic statement about his South African past and its complex heritage. More than twenty years later, the mural has become the overpowering feature of my study, and in its symmetrical design I see a person with outstretched hands and a big heart.

It is as if Sean's arms are embracing me.

I then delved into the history of the Ndebele tribe and the symbolism that had moved Sean to paint the mural.

War had broken out in 1883 between the Ndebele and the Boer Republic during the reign of their chief, Mabhoko. The Ndebele warriors defended themselves for eight long months while hiding in dark subterranean caves and tunnels in their mountain stronghold. Eventually, however, their whereabouts were discovered and the Ndebele were defeated, their world destroyed. Their tribal structure broken up and their lands confiscated, the Ndebele faced increasingly dark times, during which they also developed their own remarkable art form using geometric shapes, including squares, rectangles and triangles. The form became known as Ndebele house paintings. Through their expressive art, the Ndebele created a distinctive cultural identity that also signified their unity and survival as a people.

Their vibrant murals have become guideposts to passersby that signal: Ndebele live here.

In his choice of motif, Sean had signalled that he too had passed this way and should be remembered.

In the days to follow, I couldn't help but keep staring at the mural. I was drawn especially to the green that enveloped the heart. Green, the colour of hope. Sean had practiced yoga, meditation and Tai Chi. Green represents the heart chakra, a focal point in a variety of meditation techniques that bridge the physical and spiritual worlds, leading to greater understanding, empathy, love and compassion.

In the green field around the heart I saw an expression of Sean's hope for recovery.

Navy blue on the mural refers to the throat chakra: the centre of communication and the seat of self-expression. This chakra is a crossroad between heart and head, serving as a mediator between emotions and thoughts; the blue was the vehicle for reconnecting with Sean's true self in order to get in touch with forgotten or suppressed desire. At the same time, the colour evokes sadness, as reflected in common refrains like "feeling blue" or "singing the blues." Paradoxically, blue also exudes the warmth and tranquility of the clear blue sky.

Sean's choice of motif mirrored his fears and his striving to

discover his own identity.

A few months later, as I paged through his photograph albums, I was startled to find a faded photo of the mural with a picture of him embedded at its heart. The picture told me all I needed to know: that I had in fact understood his message. Sean had passed this way despite all obstacles—what he needed was for his passing to be acknowledged and remembered.

I continued to stare at the mural as if mesmerized. I knew the day would come when I would have to face the private world of his notebooks, sketches and journals. And one day I would. I just wasn't ready for that yet.

Months passed, and I was still sorting papers. Technically, I suppose I could have completed the task in a few weeks. But there was nothing technical about these encounters. Within an hour the files blurred and the walls closed in on me.

My refuge at those times was my study, blinds drawn. My study was my cave, my safe place, where I could recover and withdraw into the recesses of memory, and where I could review the past through the eyes of the present.

When I did return to the task of sorting, I held each and every photo, drawing, and piece of paper between my fingers, attentive to the memories.

Even with my yearning to understand my son, I realized my limits, knowing all there was to know of him. But there was something holding me back as well.

In the recesses of my mind, I kept hoping that early one morning, standing on the deck of our Muskoka cottage, watching the dark sky turn pink over the lake, I would see our canoe gliding slowly out of the receding grey mist—and there would be Sean, paddling back to us.

Rational thinking cannot compete with such yearning.

For healing to take place, I would have to journey through my loss and acknowledge the finality of death. There are few words to express this anguished state, but the Portuguese word *saudade* comes close. It describes a state of nostalgic yearning for a loved one, clouded by the sense that the person will never return. That is exactly how I felt. As I withdrew into my own darkness, I could share my grief only with Marcia. She, on the other hand, was able to share hers not only with me but with a few others as well. Friends and family urged me to speak about my feelings. Of course, I knew intellectually that sharing anguish can be a salve to the soul. But all I could do was sink into silence.

Eventually, I recalled the performance of *887* by the renowned Quebec creator and director, Robert Lepage, dealing with memory and aging in his brilliant solo portrayal. His themes resonated with me. I thought about Lepage's reminiscing about his father, recalling his life and formative years. I thought of my own father, then reversed the order of my recollections from father to son: from me to Sean, and the memories of Marcia and our other sons.

As I reviewed my own life's odyssey, the challenges I had faced gradually began to sharpen and take shape. My craft was a pen, its sails, paper. My companion at the tiller, looking forward, was Marcia, surrounded by our family. During the long journey of the Greek hero, Odysseus, it was the memories of his past that steered him home. Home for me was, at first, a distant mirage. Returning would not be easy. I knew that. But as I pressed on, I recalled Athena's admonishment to Telemachus, to find his father, Odysseus. The quest that lay before me was to find my son, Sean. What I hoped was that by digging deep into my own memories, I would link the present with the past, and in so doing, fortify myself for the future.

FOUR

The Bogeymen

The most sacred, private spaces are personal journals. I was aware of that whenever I looked at the plastic box that held Sean's private papers. I had to steel myself to open it each and every time. I felt I was intruding into his innermost thoughts, feelings, fears and hopes. Despite my reservations, I yearned to understand the terrors that attacked him.

Sean often asked about my childhood fears. I told him about the *Tokoloshe.* He smiled and said, "That's what we now call a bogeyman." He enjoyed hearing what frightened me.

When I was seven, back in the village of Hoopstad in South Africa, I remember lying in my bed in the darkened room. Suddenly I saw the *Tokoloshe* lurking at my door. I knew all about it thanks to Lizzy, our elderly cook, who had uttered threats when I stubbornly refused to eat her breakfast porridge. "If you don't eat it, the *Tokoloshe* will get you," she said. That night, unable to sleep, I stared into the dark, petrified, seeing and knowing *it* was there.

Mom came to see if I was awake. She opened the door, tucked me in, and in the semi-dark with the door ajar I could see a bear-like shape.

"There's a *Tokoloshe* in the room," I whispered, fearing evil could befall me even by mentioning its name.

She gave me a hug and squeezed me. "There is no such thing."

"It's there—there," I pointed.

She looked again. "It's only a dressing gown."

She turned on the light, and sure enough, I saw the dressing gown hanging from the door hook—that was his trick. I was right, I *had* seen him.

Lizzy was the best person to go to for advice. Our cook since Mom and Dad had arrived in Hoopstad, Lizzy herself was an imposing figure. Her black skin was wizened. A large bunch of house keys swung from a belt around her waist. Mom was too busy in the store to worry about housekeeping, which meant that Lizzy was in charge. For better or worse, being in charge meant she also told me many secrets about a world I could not see—a world Mom and Dad did not believe in—including how her ancestors spoke to her through her dreams.

"Lizzy," I told her the next day. "I saw the *Tokoloshe.* I'm afraid. What do I do?"

She bent down to me. "*Baasie*—you must be careful. Put a brick under each leg of your bed. He won't get you."

I told Mom what I needed to do.

"Where did you get that nonsense?" she asked. "There is no such thing."

What Mom didn't understand was that I'd seen it. "You'll all be sorry when it grabs me and eats me up," I cried. Still, she refused to allow me to jack up my bed with bricks.

One day when I again picked up one of Sean's notebooks, it fell open to a drawing of a greenish-brown, fearsome being with orange hair. A horn protruded from the left side of the head. Thick green branches enclosed the figure in a cage. Did the jungle branches represent his fear of haphazard wiring in his brain? As I stared at his painting, my old childhood fear resurfaced, that of the evil dwarf-like spirit, the wandering *Tokoloshe* that could pounce out of the night and attack.

On the right of the greenish-brown monster was a smaller, ferocious, brown creature with white, bared fangs. On the top right-hand corner, outside the enclosure, a skeletal face loomed in lonely isolation—a face with large ears, a nose and mouth that I later came to understand as the figure he had used to show a fearful representation of himself.

Below Sean's motif was indecipherable writing.

Much of what happened to Sean will always remain unfathomable to me.

As a child, I was lucky I had not upset the monster. It never attacked me. As an adult, I understand how the threat of the bogeyman can be used to make a child obedient, but in my childhood, fear of the bogeyman was real. For many years, I harboured a dread of the evil spirit lurking in my bedroom.

Sean was amused when I told him about another childhood fear of mine—visiting *die klein huisie* in the pitch dark outside. The village where we lived had no flush toilets. I would tiptoe behind the house and across the backyard to the outhouse, grasping my small flashlight. The narrow path of light deepened the surrounding darkness. At any time the dark shape of the monster could appear and snatch me, and I would vanish into the great black night.

Opening the creaking wooden door of the unlit outhouse, I swept the torch beam over the small space to make sure nothing lurked there that could attack me. I shone the light into the darkness of the pit below, then carefully balanced myself on the wooden toilet seat. If I didn't position my bottom properly, I would plummet into the gaping black hole.

More terrifying still was my fear that a hairy multi-clawed spider would climb up from the sewage bucket and nip out a piece of my bum.

To allay my fears, Dad often walked me to the outhouse. He would hold my hand to reassure me that nothing bad would happen. One night he said, "You see? Nothing ever happens, and I don't need to go with you."

I reminded him about the shadowy monster, the hairy spider, the looming night.

"It's okay. Nothing will happen. There's nothing there."

Mom added—often by daylight, "Don't carry on imagining such silly things."

They did not understand that I was not imagining—for me it was real.

While my childhood fears passed, sadly, Sean's did not. Carefully, I continued to turn the pages of his journal. The diary entry for November 1993 exposed another fear:

yes here's my story and it all begins about seventeen years ago when I was about a wee, few months old ... and suddenly my brother lifted me on his shoulder. He was about 4 1/2 feet taller than me at the time and all of a sudden I became about five times my height and there was something really exciting going on down the street, so there we were running together, actually it was my brother mainly running. I just panted and we ran down to where all the different fire trucks had raced to earlier and then just stopped with all the other crowd that had gathered there, and watched as some blanket was smoking. I guess they were going to smother some fire which was at the edge of the forest.

I remembered that morning. We were all safely in our townhouse at the corner of Bayview Avenue and York Mills Road, in Toronto, when we heard fire engines blaring and rushed out to join the commotion. There is nothing like big red fire engines, helmeted and thickly clad fireman unravelling the snaking white water hoses to ramp up excitement.

By the time I got there, the fire was already doused. I saw only a smoking blanket and a few patches of black grass. Little damage, thankfully.

But here, in Sean's account, was his impish humour—claiming to be a few months old, when in reality he would have been nearly four; we had arrived from South Africa just a few months before—and remembering the great thrill, sitting on Jonathan's shoulders: "We could have been for all I know in the clouds and loving it."

I read on to learn that he was shocked at our reaction when he told us about the incident many years later. According to his diary, I had said, "See look Sean you don't seem to understand we told you that it was only a little figment of your imagination and see nothing was hurt or damaged. So please that was about fifteen years ago so would you shut up already." He then continued as himself: "Ya oh. So I guess you were right. I mean hey a fire is a fire and I mean no one got hurt and I'm sure I made some of it up anyway."

I do remember him mentioning the fire, but I would never have told him to shut up. So there you go, a little hyperbole enlivens the story.

I read on:

But then tell me something. Why was [I] always ... throughout my short life worried if the house would burn down. What would be the things I must take next and if I could what I would need to run back and get and then see I became very nervous because my window happened to be on the second floor. I begged my parents to get my grandpa to make a rope that would allow me to climb down from my room in case of an emergency when the smoke would be too great to make my way through the hall of our townhouse.

Sean clearly recognized that Scott, Marcia's father, would have been the one to call on. I was definitely not the person to craft an escape makeshift ladder out of rope.

His writing, recalling his younger self, was lively and vivid. His pronounced fear of fire even at age four was palpable, and his solution, practical. I remember him telling us about it all some fifteen years later.

Reading Sean's entry about the fire reawakened the memory of my father's repeated warnings to beware of fire and water. Had I passed on Dad's fears to Sean, as part of the family folklore?

FIVE

The Crystal Jug

After Sean's passing I came to more fully appreciate the fragility of life. One minute, everything seems fine. Then something unexpected happens.

You cross the street, and a driver runs a red light.

You land in deep water unable to swim.

You stroll along the sidewalk, and a window frame falls out of a high rise.

You nod off while driving.

You trip, walking down the stairs.

You succumb to one of the many disasters that have intensified with accelerating climate change: hurricanes, tornados, tsunamis, earthquakes, fires and floods.

Then there are the health hazards humans face, from heart attacks and strokes, to influenza and the unpredictable Covid-19 pandemic that turned the world upside down.

The unexpected happens and everything changes. Forever.

One day, when I was eight years old, eating supper with my parents, Dad turned to me. "The jug's empty. Please fill it with water."

"It's too heavy for him," Mom said. "I'll do it."

The jug had been a gift he had bought, along with eight matching glasses, on a business trip to Johannesburg. With excitement, Mom unwrapped the box. "It's very special crystal made in Ireland by a famous firm called Waterford," she told me. She held the large elegant pitcher up to the light. "Look through it," she said. "It's not like ordinary glass. Feel how heavy it is."

That night, after refilling the jug in the kitchen, Mom wobbled for a second in her high-heeled shoes. The beautiful crystal pitcher flew out of her hand and smashed on the floor.

She stared at fragments of glass and pooling water, and slowly smiled. "It's only a water jug," she said.

I was lucky I hadn't dropped it. I could just hear them shouting, "Why didn't you hold it properly? Why are you so clumsy?"

Later that night, Dad comforted Mom. "Ida, don't be upset. It's only a water jug. I'll get another one when I go to Johannesburg."

Some things can be replaced. Others cannot.

One warm Sunday afternoon the family were all at Grandpa Mendel's farm, lazing on the grassy banks of the Vaal River under the shade of the fruit trees. Mom was fast asleep, lying against a tree trunk. Bees droned in the heat. One circled my face and I jumped up to swat it. Its buzzing grew louder as I furiously waved my hands.

"Let's swim across the river, get away from the bees," Uncle Mannie called out. "Come on. Climb on my back."

I hesitated, having never dared paddle more than a few feet from the river bank, where the water was no higher than my shoulders.

I looked at the calm flow of the yellow, muddy water. Brown logs that could have been mistaken for crocodiles floated by, slowly pulled by the current; they didn't frighten me. It all seemed safe. Mannie was strong, a weightlifter with big bulging muscles. He could easily swim across the river. But I didn't want to go.

"I can't swim," I said.

"It's crazy," Dad shouted.

"Julius, it's okay," the family lying on the grass replied as a chorus.

"Don't worry," Mannie said, snatching me up in his big arms and swinging me onto his back. I twirled my arms around his neck and hung on tight.

"Don't do that," Dad shouted to no avail.

Mannie jumped into the water and started swimming with powerful strokes. I clung even harder, tightening my hands around his neck. As he surged forward, muddy water splashed into my mouth. I closed my eyes, coughing, choking and sneezing. My grip began to loosen. Somehow, I couldn't stop myself from slipping off his back and sliding down into the river. My toes sank into its soft muddy bottom. There I stood frozen, underwater, for what felt like a long, long time. I did not know what to do.

Suddenly, I was scooped up.

"Are you okay?" Mannie shouted. He flipped me over his knee as if I was a small bag of potatoes and I hung there, head down, a few inches above the ground as he slapped my back, hard. I sneezed and coughed. Water spluttered out of my mouth.

"I told you so. Stupid. Stupid," Dad yelled at Mannie.

This time the family chorus was silent.

"Are you okay?" Mom cried out, holding me tight. I was still spluttering, chest heaving. Everyone clustered around me.

I shudder when I think what would have happened if Mannie hadn't pulled me out of the water.

This was my own near death experience. Drowning meant death, and death meant the end of life—a concept we, the living, find hard to fathom.

Up to the age of eight I had always wondered who Little Harry was. Granny, Mom, and Dad often mentioned his name. When I asked Mom, she told me that Little Harry was really my Uncle Harry. That was confusing. How could he still be little? And why had I never met him? She wouldn't say more.

After Grandpa Mendel died, my parents took me to the small cemetery in Bloemhof where he was buried. They placed a few pebbles on his grave and explained that the stones showed that they had been there to visit.

On our way back to the car, we stopped at a small grey tombstone with the name Harry on it. Mom placed a stone on the grave. I asked her who that was.

"This is the tombstone of your late Uncle Harry."

"What happened to him?"

"He died." Her answer seemed pretty obvious to me.

"How did he die?"

"I'll tell you later," she said as she walked towards the cemetery gate.

One day I heard Granny say to Mom, "Do you realize that Little Harry, if he was alive today, would be six years older than Henry? That would make him fourteen."

I again asked what had happened to him.

Granny said, "He died." Clearly, they didn't want to tell me more.

When I repeated my question later that night to Mom, she kept silent.

"Ida," Dad said, "I think he's old enough for you to tell him."

She then said that her baby brother, Harry, died when he was only two years old. Granny was in the passenger seat with Harry on her lap, driving back to Bloemhof with a friend, when the car door swung open as they rounded a corner. Granny and Harry were flung onto the side of the road. Harry didn't survive. Granny suffered physical injuries that she overcame, but the emotional trauma of losing her baby son remained.

Suddenly, I understood.

Those were the days before seatbelts. Granny would have been anguished at the recurring thought that had she not held him on her lap but placed him on the back seat, Harry would still be alive today.

For the rest of her life, Granny lived with the horrifying image of Harry thrown from the car, dashed against the roadside rocks. I thought of the life he had missed, the family and friends he never got to know. His future frozen in time.

Thank goodness I was quickly snatched from the muddy riverbed when I'd slipped off Uncle Mannie's back.

No one ever spoke of my near drowning.

No one said that I could now be lying next to Little Harry, and spoken of as Little Henry.

Whenever these memories surface, the lyrics of Leonard Cohen's "Who by Fire" come to mind. The song evokes the different forms of dying, speaking the unspeakable. As I recall the route Sean took, I feel the hurt once more.

SIX

Lacquering the Cracks

Dad and I were walking on the beach. I was thirteen years old. He stopped and said, "I still don't feel well. Nothing I'm doing is helping."

He had repeated this often lately. He used to shave every day, but now black-and-grey stubble sprouted on his chin.

Many years later, after Sean took his own life, my thoughts often veered towards the mental health issues in my family. I reflected on the episodes of depression and anxiety in Dad's life and on the death of my mother's uncle Max. Had the tentacles of mental anguish in Dad and Mom's families penetrated through the generations to Sean? I would never find a definitive answer, yet the question kept surfacing.

Dad returned from a visit to our family doctor. "He said I must exercise and walk every day. There's nothing he could give me to perk me up."

Mom pulled me aside. "You must go walking with Dad."

After school, on most afternoons, I drove with him in his black Chevy to Pollok Beach, a secluded area on the outskirts of the city of Port Elizabeth. We walked behind the ridge of sand dunes and green bushes on the long stretch of beautiful white sand.

He wore sandals and bent down to pull them up as they slid loose. I took mine off and squished the sand beneath my toes, careful to avoid the brown seaweed, jellyfish, broken shells and skeletons of rotting fish.

He turned to me. "World War II ended nearly five years ago. By now I thought I would've heard something about our family in Latvia. I can't find out anything. The Russians are keeping everything there closed. I wonder if any family survived. I can't stop thinking about it."

Then he said, "Let's sit down on this rock and watch the sea."

We watched the foamy waves lap the shore. I felt the spray on my face and inhaled the salt air. In the distance, a few surfers in bright swim trunks waited as a wave billowed up, then rode its crest. A school of grey bottle-nosed dolphins were springing out of the sea, arching their backs and diving down, cavorting without care.

He rose to his feet and smiled. "Watching the waves is calming."

We walked on. He put a hand on my shoulder, a signal that he was about to give me some fatherly advice.

"Even when the surface of the sea seems calm, sharks can be lurking underneath."

He started talking about Apartheid and the future of Whites in South Africa. "One day there will be a big blow-up. Apartheid can't continue. The system is cruel. A time of reckoning is coming for us Whites. I won't be here, but you will."

He paused. "Do you understand what I am telling you? I want you to be aware of what lurks out there."

He waited for an answer.

"Yes. I understand."

As we retraced our steps, I kept a careful lookout for bluebottles, the Portuguese man-o-war that looked like a battleship with a sail. As I had discovered, even when they looked dead, their deceptively thin blue threads with sharp tentacles stung as they released their poison.

In the past, Dad had always combed his hair carefully, and, as it thinned, he'd dab on a colourless oil from a small bottle.

"What's that oil?" I once asked. "It smells funny."

He laughed. "It's liquid paraffin. It keeps the hair in place. It's also good for bowel movements, so it works both ways."

All my uncles used Brylcreem. Whenever I heard the jingle "Brylcreem—A little dab'll do ya! Brylcreem—You'll look so debonaire. Brylcreem—The gals'll all pursue ya!" I thought of Dad's foul-smelling hair oil.

But now there were no jokes. His hair was ruffled, his bottle of oil in the bathroom cupboard no longer used.

He stuck to other habits faithfully and only ate what he called "healthy foods." Every morning he'd sprinkle his oatmeal porridge with blackstrap molasses and wheat germ. Then he'd swallow different coloured vitamins—brown, beige, yellow and white. There were long pills, small and round pills, and a few so big they'd have made me gag.

One afternoon I watched as he placed yogurt culture in white gauze in a large milk-filled jar. A few days later he poured out a thick white liquid. "Try it. Try it," he urged. "It's healthy. The real thing from Bulgaria. People there live a long time." I sipped a spoonful carefully, as if taking medicine, but when the sour taste of the thick liquid reached my tongue, I spluttered and spat it out. How could something that looked like toothpaste make anyone healthy? He handed me another spoonful. "It's better if you add honey."

I shook my head.

The books on his bedside table were clues to his frame of mind. There was *Look Younger, Live Longer* by Gayelord Hauser. Dad believed that Hauser's wonder foods would dispel the cloud of sadness that hung over him. He read and reread book on health, *Man Alive, You're Half Dead,* by Daniel Colin Munro, its pages stained from a spilled cup of Postum. For a bookmark, he used a blue flyer advertising another book—*I Did Not Interview the Dead* by Dr. David Pablo Boder, who interviewed survivors in displaced persons (DP) camps in Europe. "Pablo Boder is a cousin," Dad explained. "He knew our family in Libau. He was lucky—he left Europe before the Nazi invasion. He's smart and became a professor of psychology in Chicago."

I was struck by the word "dead" in the two book titles. Dr. Boder visited the DP camps after the war to interview the traumatized, survivors. He wanted to keep alive the truth of their suffering and the memory of those who, tragically, could no longer be interviewed. Munro's book, by contrast, emphasized keeping people physically alive, even if they were already half dead, thanks to having ignored the choices for healthy living.

The books Dad devoured on health, the countless vitamins he swallowed and his daily exercise regimen did not improve his well-being. He woke in the mornings bleary-eyed, seldom smiled, and spoke only when asked a question. His hair was unkempt and he often wore the same clothes for days on end until Mom urged him to change.

The conversations on our walks now revolved around the horrors of the war and the loss of his family. If it were not for Mom insisting that he go for his daily walk, he would have remained in the apartment listening to the radio, reading *The Eastern Provence Herald*, our local newspaper, or sitting in his comfortable chair in the lounge, staring at the carpet.

Mom took him to see a doctor again. A series of appointments followed. "We've been told he's having a nervous breakdown and that he needs shock treatment," she said a few weeks later. I had no idea what that meant. "They will put electrodes on his scalp and apply electric shocks," she explained.

"Won't the electric shocks electrocute him?" I asked, horrified. I told her about a photo I'd seen of a prisoner in America being put to death by electrocution. He was strapped into an electric chair, electrodes attached to his head.

"It's not like that. It'll definitely help him." She put her arm around me and gave me a big hug. "We must try it. Nothing else has helped."

I was still frightened. I also felt that she was not convinced but did not want me to be concerned.

He told me later, "There's nothing else. I can't go on like this."

My parents travelled to Johannesburg for Dad's treatment. I stayed with friends and joined them two weeks later. The train trip was a long, overnight journey. Mom managed to find someone to accompany me. I was thrilled by the train's charging forward, then swaying gently from side to side. I sat on the green leather seat of the compartment and peered out the window, fixated on the passing landscape—mountain ranges, fields of crops, white-walled farmhouses with red roofs, cattle, pastures dotted with sheep and horses grazing. Speeding cars sprayed clouds of dust on the gravel roads that ran beside the railway tracks.

Yet underneath my excitement, I was apprehensive about how the therapy had affected Dad. What would I find when I arrived in Johannesburg?

Mom and I stayed with Granny Sarah's brother Max, a widower. Even though his house was outside the city, he or his son drove us to the private hospital to see Dad.

What a sight he was. Pale, his hair untidy, he was lying on the bed wearing the grey dressing gown he had brought with him. He smiled broadly when I walked in. I leaned over and gave him a big hug. After that initial greeting, his smile faded and he hardly spoke. I asked him about the treatment. All he said, "It was okay." He wouldn't say more.

Mom and I stayed a few hours every day. There wasn't much to talk about and nothing I could really do at the hospital.

Max, our host, was kind. He offered cake and candies. Luckily for me, he had an old set of leather-bound *Encyclopedia Britannica* filled with pictures and interesting facts. Otherwise, I would have been bored out of my mind.

After our return to Port Elizabeth, Dad was more subdued. I asked him again what it was like to have had the treatment. "I don't remember much of what happened. I'm not sure if it really helped."

Our long afternoon walks on the beach, just the two of us, became a thing of the past.

Dad moved *I Did Not Interview the Dead* from his bedside table to the back of his closet, as if he never wanted to see the book again. He still kept eating oatmeal porridge with molasses and wheat germ for breakfast, and swallowing a great assortment of vitamins. Otherwise, he kept to himself in the apartment.

One of the few outings he still enjoyed was walking in the summer evenings. The three of us strolled along the Humewood Promenade that bordered the beach to a cafeteria known as the Dollorico, for tea and scones. To the west of the cafe was a ravine called Happy Valley, where at night during the summer months, festive coloured lights brightened the walkways. I never grew tired of the fairyland valley and the vervet monkeys with their black faces, white fringes of hair and grizzled-grey bodies. Often, they'd jump out of the bush, and I'd feel a surge of excitement, waiting to see if they would grab someone's handbag, or sparkling costume jewelry, or worse still, my ice cream cone.

As we walked, he never lost an opportunity to offer advice. "Beware of all the monkeys in the trees. There are many different sly monkeys out there in the world." I knew that he wasn't only referring to vervet monkeys.

Whenever he started talking about his family in Europe, Mom would intervene. "Julius, it's not good for you to talk about it all the time." Then she would look at me. "What did you do at school today?" I enjoyed telling them what had happened at school but froze when they commented that I should spend more time on homework.

I knew Dad feared for his family, yet still I wondered why he continued to be so depressed and anxious. Maybe there was another reason; maybe their money was running out. When we lived in Hoopstad, they had owned a large store, but here in Port Elizabeth neither of my parents worked. If their money ran out, we would have to move out of our apartment into a tent at the local campground. I was embarrassed to ask about money. I didn't know how to put the question casually.

One evening as we walked along the Promenade I blurted out, "What are we going to do when all your money is gone?"

They looked at me in surprise. At first, neither of them said a thing.

"We're comfortable," Mom said, "Don't worry. We have enough."

I felt better when they both smiled broadly, seemingly unconcerned.

"You have to live within your means," Dad added quickly. "You have to know the difference between need and want."

"We live quietly," Mom added.

I knew what her remark meant. They enjoyed going to the beach, swimming in the sea, taking walks, listening to the radio, reading and getting together with friends. They rarely went to the movies. There was only one restaurant at the time in the city, Chez Victor, and they seldom went there. "It's just wasting money," Mom would say.

Whenever Dad met a wealthy businessman older than himself, someone who hadn't yet retired, he would say to me, "What does he think? He can take it with him in the box?"

I marvelled that my parents' happiness did not depend on acquiring more money or possessions. Their quality of life was not tied to material things.

Dad often repeated, "We want you to benefit from our experience."

As I call to mind my meaningful talks with Dad, I think of the times shared with Sean and my three other sons. Our being together usually related more to activities—going to a zoo or a museum, enjoying the beach, watching a movie, taking a drive, and travelling overseas. If only I had spent hours exchanging hopes, dreams, and reflections on life rather than going on outings together.

We never saw Max again. One day Mom received a phone call from his son, Harry, saying Max had been killed in a train accident. His car had stalled on the railway track. I asked what had happened, but she kept quiet. She had been crying. He was her last surviving uncle.

A few months later, she said, "It's crazy that the railways are demanding payment from Max's estate for damage to the train. They think it wasn't a real accident."

I was surprised she hadn't told me before that he had possibly taken his own life. "Why would he do such a thing?" I asked.

"Uncle Max had financial problems. All very sad," she said. She looked away. Already she had told me more than she'd wanted to.

Over the years I often thought about him. His car hadn't stalled—he had intentionally stopped on the railway tracks. I felt sorry that Max, who had been kind to me, was so desperate about his finances that he'd felt compelled to take his own life.

Friends being friends, they gave Dad well-meaning advice about what he should do to feel better. "Julius, you retired too early. You should go back into business. It will keep your mind occupied."

He started looking into buying a business. A steady stream of vendors soon appeared, offering stores for sale—everything from furniture, grocery, cafeterias, and bicycle repairers to book shops. He listened to all the sales pitches and finally decided he didn't want to purchase any of them. "A fool and his money are soon parted," he said. That closed the door on the subject.

Mom then said, "Julius, do you remember during the war when there was no new furniture available, you went to Johannesburg and bought broken furniture and repaired it?"

He nodded.

"Why don't you start a business like that here?"

He smiled and shook his head. Later I realized that he had thought further about her suggestion.

One afternoon Dad came home with an assortment of materials for woodwork: a plane, a saw, screwdrivers, pliers, sandpaper and glue.

"What are you doing Julius? Do you want to become a carpenter?" Mom teased.

"I have to do something with my hands," he answered without smiling.

Next morning he rose early. "I'm going to a furniture auction at Vigne & Howard," he announced. Mom looked surprised. "I'm going to buy some broken antique pieces to fix. They usually go for next to nothing."

A few hours later, he unloaded broken furniture from the trunk and backseat of his Chevy into the apartment's enclosed back porch. Mom did not comment. After lunch he donned his oldest clothes and started scraping off the old paint from a broken antique table. He sandpapered the wood, stuck the table back together and brushed on brown liquid from a jam jar.

"What's that?" I asked as I smelled the pungent liquid. He explained that it was called shellac, made from resin secreted by the female lac bug found on trees in the forests of India and Thailand. He used it as a stain to get a high-gloss varnish on the wood.

"Feel here," he said. I ran my fingers over the table-top's smooth, glossy finish. The shellac had sealed all the cracks and evened out the roughness of the wood.

I have often thought of him retreating to his improvised workshop on the back balcony of our apartment. After a few hours in his shellac-stained clothes, he'd emerge proud that he had restored another piece of antique furniture. As he became engrossed in this hobby, he seldom spoke about the family in Latvia. He had found a purpose to fill his day.

Sean, in his latter years, was unable to do so.

Looking back, I think Dad had built a shell around himself that helped protect him from the anguish of his loss.

Neither my son, Sean, nor my great-uncle, Max, was able to protect himself from anxiety. For them, there was no protective shell.

SEVEN

Frieda

Frieda Horwitz often disappeared for days on end. She would withdraw into her apartment, pull down the blinds and surface two weeks later. Mom and Dad would wonder if they had said something to upset her. Then she would suddenly appear, smiling cheerfully, as if nothing had happened. At last, my parents realized that whatever had prompted Frieda's temporary absence, it was nothing they had done.

"I suppose that's what she's like," Dad said. "She's strange."

To me, at the age of eleven, the word *strange* just meant *unusual.* It was only many years later that I understood the deeper meaning.

Frieda was Mom's best friend and lived in an adjoining apartment. I thought she was a widow as she often spoke of her late husband, but Dad later told me that her husband had left her. Frieda, who was much older than Mom, was short and overweight, with grey streaking her black hair. She usually surfaced at ten o'clock in the morning, and for the next two hours she walked around without makeup, hair in blue curlers, dressed in her pink fluffy gown. I was fascinated by her matching pink slippers, each topped with a small white mouse with black whiskers and tiny, red glass-button eyes.

In our first year in Port Elizabeth, Mom relied heavily on Frieda for advice: where to buy the freshest fish, the best price for vegetables, choosing a dressmaker, hairdresser, doctor and even a dentist. They spent hours sitting on the balcony facing the sea, sipping cups of tea and chatting.

Frieda often asked me about my day and offered me cookies and lemonade. I began to think of her as a lonely elderly aunt. I enjoyed talking to her about school and the exciting books I was reading. One day I shared with her how I would become a great racing-car driver. She in turn told me little about herself. What she gave me, though, was real insight into life. Everyone needs a kindly aunt, and she became mine. We weren't related but that was not important.

Soon after we arrived in Port Elizabeth, a throbbing toothache started keeping me awake at nights. The cloves Mom gave me to suck didn't help.

Frieda arrived with an immediate solution. "My dentist is wonderful. The best. Very experienced." So Mom made an appointment. Frieda insisted on coming with us to make, as she said, a proper introduction.

Inside the building, Frieda guided us to the elevator. It was barely big enough for the three of us. This being my first ride, I hesitated to step in. Frieda, though, was fearless. She flung open the brass gate, slammed it with a bang and pushed a yellowed button on the control panel. We stood back and waited. When nothing happened, she yanked the gate open, pulled it back till it locked with a click, and jammed the button with her thumb. Again, nothing moved.

Mom frowned. “Don’t you think it’s safer to take the stairs? It’s only one flight.”

Frieda opened and closed the metal gate with increasing fury, banging it more loudly each time. She repeatedly pressed the yellowed button, muttering, “What’s wrong with it?” Finally, the elevator gave a jerk and shuddered to the next floor. I worried the cab would collapse and we would all fall into the pit below.

“You have to know how to handle it.” Frieda was flushed but smiling as she opened the gate. I couldn’t understand why she made such a fuss about getting it to work; we could easily have walked up the flight of steps.

Mom was not impressed, and kept her lips tightly closed. As soon as the elevator stopped, she yanked the heavy door open and I jumped out.

This was my first visit to a dentist, and I didn’t know what to expect. The reception area reeked of antiseptic, and the blue lines on the shiny white linoleum floor had faded from scrubbing. Frieda rang a small brass bell on a wooden table. An old man in an oversized white coat with a few scraggly white hairs on his balding head emerged from a side room and shuffled up to us. His shoulders were stooped. He recognized Frieda immediately and smiled at her.

“This is Dr. Atkinson,” she said. He squinted at Mom and me through his steel-rimmed glasses, trying to work out which of us was his new patient. “This is my friend Ida and her son, Henry. He has a toothache. I told them you were the best dentist in Port Elizabeth.” She and the doctor laughed.

Dr. Atkinson looked ancient. I wondered if all dentists were that old. A woman who seemed older than Frieda hovered in the background. She too wore a white coat, and looked like a nurse.

He led me to his dental chair. I climbed onto its yellowed leather seat as the nurse handed him a pointed metal rod. “Open wide,” he said. He tapped and prodded my teeth, squinting at the small mirror that he stuck in my mouth. “Ah, as I thought. A small cavity.” He pulled down a lever with a drill end.

"Aren't you going to give him an injection?" Mom asked.

"No, I don't believe in injections. The needle could damage the nerve."

Frieda nodded in agreement.

He furiously pumped a foot pedal and the drill whizzed and whined. Whenever he touched the cavity, my jaw vibrated with pain. "Ouch," I shouted. He stopped for a few seconds, then carried on. I clutched the armrests, wondering how long the torture would continue.

I walked out of that office, a dull pain throbbing in my mouth. It was better, I concluded, to have a toothache than to go to the dentist.

When we got home, Mom told Dad, "That dentist and his equipment should be in a museum."

"I don't know why Frieda goes to him," Dad said. "Maybe he's good at fixing her dentures."

Mom pulled a face. "Frieda acted weird. You should've seen how mad she got at the clunky old elevator. She didn't seem all right to me."

Many years later I wondered if "weird" and "didn't seem all right" were code words for Mom's concern that Frieda's behaviour was more than eccentricity. She was not well.

That night, after my visit to Dr. Atkinson, I again woke with a toothache. Mom said we should go back to see him in the morning. The idea frightened me but she was adamant. She added, "I don't need Frieda to come with us and get agitated."

He again peered into my mouth, prodding with the metal stick. "There's no other cavity," he said. "Suck some cloves and it will go away."

"Aren't you going to give him an X-ray, to see if there's a cavity?" she asked.

"No, I don't believe in X-rays. They can be dangerous."

Mom swallowed her surprise and watched apprehensively as he poked around my mouth.

He drew her aside into the reception area and whispered, "I'm absolutely sure there's nothing wrong with his teeth. There's no cavity. It's definitely his nerves."

On the way back home, Mom strode fast. "What sort of dentist is he, saying it's your nerves? Does he think you're crazy?" She stopped walking and turned to me. "I'm sorry, I didn't mean anything about being crazy. You're absolutely fine. It's just him talking nonsense."

That afternoon I heard Mom tell Frieda, "How dare he say it was Henry's nerves?"

Frieda glowered at Mom. "He's been my dentist for over forty years. He knows what he's talking about. He's not like all those young dentists with new-fangled ideas—their fancy electric drills, injections, X-rays. They don't know the damage they're doing."

"Well," Dad said, "he might have plenty of experience, but he's not up to date." Being up to date was important to him.

Frieda glared at him. Then she turned again to Mom. "It's Henry's nerves. Maybe he's got a nervous disposition," she whispered.

Mom's cheeks flushed red.

I was intrigued by the word "disposition." I did not know what it meant but I felt important that at least I had one. Then again, I would have been happier if it weren't also giving me a toothache.

We changed dentists. After an X-ray the cavity was found, and the tooth filled painlessly, thanks to an injection. Not surprisingly, my toothache disappeared.

But the idea that I had a "nervous disposition" troubled me, reminding me of an incident that happened three years earlier when I was eight years old.

One night after Christmas, while we were still living in Hoopstad, I heard screaming coming from the police station; it was only one building away from our house. I asked Mom what was happening.

"There's a poor woman locked up in a cell, crying," Mom said.

"Did she steal anything or murder anyone?" I asked.

"No. She had a nervous breakdown and they're taking her to a mental asylum in Bloemfontein. Maybe she's hungry."

Mom went to the kitchen and cut two thick slices of bread and made a chicken sandwich and a mug of coffee. "We're taking her something to eat," Mom said. "Stay here and go to sleep."

I quietly followed my parents into the backyard of the police station. There was no guard. I heard the woman cry, *"Laat my uit. Laat my uit."* She wanted to be let out. In a soothing voice, Mom said that tomorrow she would be taken to a hospital, where they would look after her. Then she offered the sandwich and coffee. The woman stopped crying and thanked her.

I hurried back to the house and dove into bed. I lay awake most of that night thinking of the cruelty of locking up a crying woman just because she had what Mom called a nervous breakdown.

I had heard of mumps, whooping cough and measles but had never heard of a "nervous breakdown."

As a teenager, in moments of unhappiness or self-doubt, I would worry that Frieda and the dentist had been right about me. Eventually I dismissed the thought and saw their words—"his nerves" and "nervous disposition"—in a different light. *This was labelling.*

One evening when I was twelve, I heard my parents whispering outside my room. "No, you go and tell him. It's your job, you're the father."

Dad came into my room and sat down, looking sheepish. "Do you know where you came from?" he asked.

I was puzzled—didn't he know? "Yes, from Hoopstad."

He smiled. I knew it was the wrong answer. "No, I mean how you were born."

"What would you like to know?" I asked, not sure how detailed an answer he wanted. "I know all about it."

"Are you sure?" Before I could answer he said, "Okay. That's good." Looking relieved, he quickly left my room unaware of my vast knowledge of the subject.

My parents would have been horrified had they realized how much I knew about sex and how I had found out. I knew more about sex than all my friends put together and maybe even their parents, thanks to a gift from Frieda—a set of six, thick volumes wrapped in brown paper, which I later realized was not meant to keep the books clean but to hide their titles.

That gift would turn out to be one of the best presents I'd ever received.

"Have you thought of becoming a doctor?" Frieda had asked me one day.

I wasn't surprised by the question. She had asked me that before. I never understood why no one ever asked me if I wanted to become a plumber, a pharmacist, an accountant or even a lawyer. "I don't know," I said. "There's still lots of time."

"I just remembered," she said, "I want to give you a lovely set of books my late husband bought. He wanted to become a doctor but never did. Perhaps if you read them, you'll want to be a doctor one day." She heaved herself out of her comfortable chair, shuffled over to the bookcase on the other side of the room and pulled out a pile of books, each wrapped in plain brown paper. "I tried reading them but it wasn't for me. You can keep them."

Back in my bedroom I noticed the name of the author, Havelock Ellis. I had never heard of him. Then I saw the title, *Studies in the Psychology of Sex*. That meant something. I became so engrossed in reading that I devoured all six volumes and became a speed reader. That set of books opened a new world to me.

As a twelve-year-old boy I had been transported by C.S. Forester's series of books on the heroic deeds of Captain Horatio Hornblower and his rise in the ranks of the Royal Navy from lieutenant to admiral. The books from Frieda were different. Here I was blown away. Most of what I read I had never heard discussed by anyone, boy or adult. Before these volumes, anything I'd wanted to discover about sex I'd had to piece together from rumour and innuendo from friends, who also knew very little. And while I shared my new-found knowledge with my friends, I did not divulge my source. They would have asked to borrow the books. I could well imagine the shock on their parents' faces if they discovered their sons reading volume after volume devoted to sex.

The books Frieda gave me not only kept me fully engrossed for months, they broadened my thinking. Havelock Ellis was a progressive physician who had set out to challenge the taboos and hypocrisies embedded in Victorian society. His work helped to pave the way for the greater openness of the modern era.

I also realized how unusual it was for Frieda to give me those books. I wondered how much she knew of their contents, despite her claim that they were "not for her." Maybe she'd drawn from her own life experience and wanted to open my mind to ideas that at the time lay outside the prudery that may well have constricted her own life.

"What are those books in the brown paper covers about?" Dad asked me one day as he wandered into my room.

"Oh. They're just some old books Frieda gave me," I said casually. I was afraid he might open one of the volumes. I had no idea how he would react. And more, this treasure trove—and the knowledge it represented—was my own dark secret, and mine alone.

"Where's Frieda?" I asked Mom one morning. I was eighteen and hadn't seen her for a while.

"She's not well."

"But where is she?"

Mom didn't answer. I repeated the question.

"She's in Grahamstown," Mom said, looking down.

I was surprised, for I knew what that meant. Grahamstown was a small university town about an hour's drive from Port Elizabeth, but "being in Grahamstown" was a euphemism for the Fort England Hospital, formerly called the Grahamstown Lunatic Asylum. Mom's reluctance to talk about it reflected the taboos and lack of awareness surrounding mental illness at the time.

I saw Frieda as an eccentric but kind elderly lady, who always had time to speak to me and had taken an interest in my future. I had to visit her and find out why she was there.

I drove to Fort England Hospital on my own. The former army barracks had been taken over from the military for use as a civilian hospital. Some of the older buildings had thick walls and narrow-slit windows, which gave the place a forbidding, defensive look. The whole complex made me feel sad. I thought of the time when patients suffering from mental illness had to be strictly guarded and restrained in a straitjacket.

I asked to see Frieda.

"Who are you?" asked a thin-faced woman. She sat near the front door at a desk, behind a typewriter. Her greying hair was pulled tightly into a bun.

"I'm a friend. Tell her Henry, Ida's son, wants to see her."

She looked at me quizzically, unsure if she should let me in. "She doesn't get many visitors. I'll have to find out if she wants to see you." Pointing to the waiting room, she asked me to remain there.

I slipped into a large room filled with frayed sofas, rickety tables, mismatched chairs and small vases stuffed with plastic flowers that I imagined were meant to enliven the place. Faded landscape prints, some behind glass and others bulging from frames with rust-covered stains, hung slightly askew on the cracked and peeling yellow-painted walls.

A few people were sitting on their own. Some were slouched in their chairs and seemed heavily drugged. I assumed they were patients. One stared at me, wondering, I suppose, whom I had come to visit. Or was I a new patient waiting to be admitted? A woman entered through the front door and a patient jumped up, rushed towards her, and burst out crying as they embraced.

A slender elderly lady in a baggy yellow dress, with a heavily lined face, sunken cheeks, and no teeth, came up to me. "Welcome young man," she said. "My name is Agnes." She stuck out her arm. When I shook her bony hand, she quickly pulled it back. "You're young to be here, but don't worry. We've got nice doctors and I'm sure you'll be okay. In no time you'll be out of here," she said, eyeing me intently.

"I'm not a patient. I'm just waiting to see someone."

"Really. So. You can't fool me. I know you're waiting to be admitted." Then she scowled. "You don't have to be embarrassed—we're all in the same position here." She shuffled away.

Three-quarters of an hour had passed. I went back to the woman at reception. She was busy flipping through a magazine. "Will she be able to see me?" I asked.

"She'll be here soon," the woman said.

"Does anyone ever come to visit her?"

"She doesn't usually get visitors. Sometimes a rabbi comes around. Her daughter has come. And there's a man and woman from Port Elizabeth who bring her fresh clothes and things."

I knew it must be my parents. I was pleased they visited but surprised they never told me about it. I had yet to understand the stigma and silence enveloping mental illness.

"She'll be here soon," the woman said again. "She's trying to make herself look good. That's not so easy." The woman smiled. "Most patients here don't get visitors. People sort of forget about them." She pointed to a small man in a large brown armchair in the corner of the room. "That man never gets visitors."

I walked over to him. He was slumped in his chair, unshaven, with long dishevelled hair. He was staring at the carpet, fixated.

"Hullo," I said, standing before him. He slowly raised his head and looked at me in surprise. He said nothing. "My name's Henry."

"Thank you, young man, for saying hullo. It's nice of you," he mumbled softly. Suddenly, an orderly came up to him. "Excuse me—I must go, the doctor wants to see me. Thank you again for saying hullo." The man slowly lifted himself out of the chair and ambled away.

Another orderly appeared. This one held Frieda by the arm. She was pale, with no makeup other than a streak of bright red lipstick. Her hair had turned snowy white. She wore a loose-fitting grey dress. Her old pink slippers now had only one small white mouse. This was not the well-dressed Frieda I remembered.

She peered around the room and as she recognized me, smiled, and waved with her free hand. "So nice of you to come all the way to see me," she said as I approached her. I hugged her, and smelled the strong odour of talcum powder. She shuffled to the couch, sat next to me and leaned in close. "Do you know why I'm here?" Before I could reply she moved closer and said in a low voice, "I'm writing a book about the terrible conditions in this place. They don't know it; that's why I'm here." She leaned back. "Please keep it to yourself—it's a secret. Don't tell anyone, not even Ida or Julius. If people here find out, they'll kick me out."

I promised to keep her secret. "I look forward to reading the book—it's important, people should know," I said in a whisper, also leaning towards her. I knew she was embarrassed, wanting me to believe that she was only there to do research. Trying to lighten the mood, I pointed to her shorn slipper. "That mouse must have run away. Is the other one lonely?"

She looked down at her slipper and smiled. "Funny, I hadn't noticed. Everyone, I think, is lonely here."

"Have you made friends?"

"No. There's lots of people here, but no one to talk to. They all have their own problems. I can't bear to hear them complain about children who don't visit them, horrible dreams that keep them awake, and screams they hear in the middle of the night. They repeat all the time that they just don't know why their family stuck them in this place. I have my own problems to think about." Her sentences bubbled out. "The food's terrible and it gets bitterly cold in winter—no proper heating. But it's not so bad for me, I'll be leaving soon."

When I left I gave her a big hug. I was upset that she was mentally ill and that she was living in such depressing conditions. As I drove home, I remembered her many quirky habits that we hadn't understood at the time. I realized how little we had really known about Frieda.

She would remain "in Grahamstown" until the end of her life.

Many years later, I received a phone call inviting me to be on the board of a psychiatric hospital foundation in Toronto. "Yes," I said spontaneously.

"Do you know what it's all about?" The caller asked, taken aback by my immediate response.

"Yes, I think I know."

As a teenager I could not do much for Frieda, but as an adult I hoped that I could perhaps do some good for someone else who might be suffering. I did not know then how life would unfold.

EIGHT

Sunday Morning

Often when I think of Sean I recall a Sunday morning while I was still a law student in Cape Town. The shrill ringing of the phone in the passage startled me awake. I stared into the darkness of my bedroom.

"It's not even seven. Henry's asleep," I heard Ronnie, my roommate, say. He was a medical student who got up at six every morning to study. He tapped on my bedroom door before opening it. "There's a guy called Issy on the phone. He wants to talk to you. Says it's urgent." Ronnie placed his hand over the receiver and whispered, "He seems a bit strange."

"What does he want?" I didn't want to speak to Issy or anyone else at that hour, and I'd just seen him the night before. We'd been on a double date. He was silent most of the evening, appearing dazed and distant. He hardly spoke to his companion.

"What's it about?" Ronnie asked. After a moment, his hand again over the mouthpiece—"He says he's committed suicide."

I jumped out of bed and grabbed the phone. "What's happened?"

"I committed suicide," Issy said in a hoarse voice.

I felt confused. How could he still be speaking? "What did you do?"

"I took strychnine."

"Issy says he took strychnine," I whispered to Ronnie.

"In that case he's already dead. Strychnine works quickly." Ronnie's matter-of-fact tone betrayed his irritation. His study routine had been interrupted.

For an instant, I thought it might be a bad joke, but Issy sounded desperate. "Stay there," I shouted, "I'll come right over."

Dressing hurriedly, I ran down the stairs to my car, raced over to his apartment, and charged up the stairs. I was not about to wait for the elevator. The door to Issy's place stood ajar. A police officer loomed in the entrance. Issy was standing behind him in a yellow dressing gown, spattered with blood.

The officer turned towards me and with a strong Afrikaans accent said, "We must get him to emergency quickly. Can't wait for the ambulance. Can you take him in your car?"

"It'll be much quicker in the police car," I said.

"Ja, but my tunic has just been dry-cleaned and I don't want to get blood on it."

I thought his comment absurd.

I bundled Issy in his blood-spattered gown into my red Fiat 1100. The police car led the way with the siren off since it was Sunday with little traffic. We raced along Main Road to Groote Schuur Hospital, which was near my apartment in Rosebank.

Issy sat quietly. When I asked him what had happened, he did not answer but only stared fixedly at the road, as if in a trance. Blood oozed from his arm and chest onto the seat and floor. Whenever I touched the brakes, he lurched forward.

At the hospital entrance the officer pushed Issy into a wheelchair. A white-coated orderly rushed out, looked at Issy, and said, "We have to stop the bleeding immediately."

This was my first visit as an adult to a public hospital. I was bewildered, seeing people pushing wheelchairs, wobbling around on crutches, being carried on stretchers. Others walked slowly, bags of liquid hanging from metal poles and tubes attached to their arms.

In the waiting room I dwelled on what Issy had done. There seemed to be so much going for him. He was intelligent, well-spoken, tall, and according to my perception, handsome. Unlike many other students, he had the financial resources to live in a large apartment, own a car and buy a substantial collection of law books. He should be looking forward to a promising career as a lawyer.

This was the first time someone I knew tried to take his own life. Many years later, faced with my son's depression and paranoia, I would learn that mental illness can affect anyone—even apparently highly successful people or acclaimed celebrities. Success and wealth provide no impermeable shield against the trauma of mental illness.

The hours dragged by. An older man and woman came in, glanced at me and took a seat. I asked them if they were Issy's parents, and they nodded. I introduced myself as his law school classmate and told them I had brought him to the hospital. His father told me in a Russian accent that Issy had called them at five o'clock that morning, sounding desperate and confused, asking them to come to him immediately. They had dashed to the airport and had taken the first flight into Cape Town from Johannesburg.

"What happened?" they asked anxiously. I described in detail all I had done that morning. Issy's father was tall, well-built, unshaven with a thick shock of greying black hair. He brought to mind a Russian aristocrat. As I spoke, he listened grim-faced. Issy's mother was dressed in dark grey, her black hair streaked with white. She wore no makeup. She was frantic.

"Do you know why he did this?" she asked.

I shook my head. There was no point in telling them about his strange behaviour the previous night.

After the cinema, on our double date, I had suggested going for coffee.

Issy leaned forward from the back seat of my car and said, "I have a terrible headache. I feel horrible. Would you mind taking me home first, before Susan?"

His date looked surprised, then she nodded. "Issy was weird tonight," Susan said to my date and me later as I drove her home.

"Why, what did he do?" I asked.

"He didn't do anything. It's like he wasn't there with us at all."

In the waiting room, his father asked me who I was, where I came from, how long I had known Issy and if I was a good friend. I could only say that we knew each other from law school.

I looked around the hospital, a world unknown to me, peopled by white-coated, stethoscope-bedecked doctors who examined patients, glanced at charts, nodded and smiled. Every word they uttered was received as if spoken by an oracle.

Nurses in starched white uniforms strode in and out, while attendants cleaned surfaces and whisked away garbage.

Issy's mother paced up and down, softly repeating, "Why?"

His father sat, head down, wringing his hands. "Rosa, please sit down. There's nothing we can do. We have to wait to hear how the operation is going."

Three hours later the surgeon appeared, still dressed in his surgical gown. Issy's parents rushed towards him.

"We stitched him together okay," the surgeon said, "but I'm not sure if we can get rid of the poison."

His mother raised her arms as if in prayer. "Doctor. Doctor. Whatever you need ... blood, bone, marrow, anything ... whatever you need, you can take it from me." Her beseeching voice bordered on hysteria. The surgeon backed away, as if not knowing how to respond to a mother whose son had slashed himself, taken poison, and was lying drugged in the recovery room.

"Rosa. Rosa. Please be a *mensch*," her husband said sternly. He seemed embarrassed at her outburst.

Issy seemed to recover from his frenzied cutting and stabbing, and after a few days the doctor said there was a chance he would recover from the poisoning as well. Finally, I was allowed to see him.

"Thank you for rushing me to the hospital," Issy said, breathing with difficulty. "I phoned other people before you. They thought I was crazy, maybe I was. I also called the police."

"Why did you do it?" I asked.

"I couldn't disappoint my parents again after all they've done for me. But I feel terrible when I see how upset they are. I hope I'll pull through."

Issy's mother and father stayed around the clock, sleeping at night in chairs in his room. They looked exhausted—his father with grey stubble, his clothing creased and crumpled, his mother pale, her hair dishevelled. She kept asking the doctor if Issy would recover.

"We're doing our best. Things are promising." That was the best she could get out of the doctor.

Issy mumbled to me one afternoon, "I want to live."

"You will," I answered emphatically.

I first met Issy at the Hiddingh Hall Library of the Cape Town law school one night while searching for a particular law report. We were both in the same class. To my surprise, he offered me the use of his personal law library. He said he had full sets of law reports and all the law books he needed in his apartment. I thought he was exaggerating, but when I later visited him, I found his library was bigger than that of the law firm where I worked.

"Why have you bought so many books?" I asked.

"Well," he said, "I didn't do well at law school in Johannesburg. I couldn't concentrate. There were too many distractions." He came here, he said, to get away from home and friends, and study without interruption. "My parents let me buy all these books so I can get through."

I looked around at the large two-bedroom apartment he occupied on his own. It was bigger than the one Ronnie and I shared.

"How are the studies going?" I asked.

"Not too well. I did lousy in yesterday's corporate law exam. I can't understand it. You did much better than me, and you're working during the day, doing the degree part-time."

I tried to reassure him that it was only a minor test. He shouldn't take it seriously.

Issy stayed silent and then said, "I studied through the night for two nights before the exam, drinking lots of coffee and taking pills to keep awake, and I still didn't do well. I don't know if I'm going to make it."

"What are these small round pills?" I pointed to a bottle on the table.

"Ritalin, a stimulant. After what my parents have done for me and all they've spent, they'll be terribly disappointed if I don't get through."

As I sat in his hospital room with Issy's parents, I felt sure he'd recover. He desperately wanted to live. After ten days, the doctors seemed hopeful as well.

Two days later, on my next visit to the hospital, I found an empty bed. I assumed Issy had been discharged or moved to another ward.

"Where is Issy?" I asked the nurse cleaning out the room.

"He died," she said softly.

"What? Are you sure?"

She said his body had been taken away early that morning. That was all she knew.

I rushed over to the hotel where his parents were staying.

His mother hugged me, crying. "Why did he do it?"

I had no answer.

"The doctor said it was the poison that did it," his father said softly, staring at the carpet.

Issy's burial was my first funeral. I did not know what to expect. I had difficulty finding the Maitland Cemetery and was concerned it would appear I didn't care enough to be on time. I climbed out of my car, buttoned my coat against the biting winter wind and followed a gravel pathway past rows of grey-and-black granite and marble tombstones. I kept walking until I saw Issy's parents. They were standing with a small group, near a hearse.

"We want you to be a pallbearer," his father said. He drew a black skullcap out of his pocket and put it on my head.

A man in a black coat and hat walked up to me and introduced himself as the rabbi. I watched, surprised, as he pulled out a small pocketknife from his jacket, opened the blade, and approached Issy's father, who unbuttoned his coat and jacket. The rabbi made a small tear on the left side of the shirt. Issy's father put his forefinger in the hole and ripped the shirt further. The traditional rending of the garment over the heart reflected the broken heart within it.

I was the only student from our law class. A man was holding Issy's mother, who was sobbing into his shoulder. She noticed me through her tears and beckoned me to come over. She introduced the man as her other son.

An undertaker in a dark overcoat asked a few of the men, myself included, to come to the black hearse. A plain pine coffin lay in the back. Two more undertakers manoeuvred the coffin out of the hearse. One of them showed me which handle to hold. I lifted my side carefully and we all filed to the gravesite. I staggered on the uneven grass, then righted myself, afraid I would stumble and fall. The scene was surreal; I was unable to accept the fact that Issy's body was inside the coffin, yet of course I knew it was.

At the graveside, we slowly set the coffin down and I rubbed my hands to dull the ache from carrying the heavy load, both physical and emotional.

The rabbi, after asking the mourners to gather around, intoned prayers in Hebrew and English. Issy's father and brother recited the Kaddish, the memorial prayer for the dead. Two of the undertakers positioned the coffin over the freshly dug hole and started to lower it into the ground.

I looked around and saw a barrister I'd once met at court. I knew him only as Advocate Berman. He greeted me with a wan smile. I joined him and his wife at the back of the group of mourners and said, "This is the first funeral I have ever been to. Maybe I shouldn't be so near to the grave in case I faint and fall in."

They both smiled.

When a scraping sound came from the grave, I stepped forward and peered down. The coffin lid, wedged against the walls, was opening.

"Oh my God," someone screamed.

The gravediggers heaved the coffin out and jumped into the hole, spades in hand, to enlarge the grave.

"Leave me. Leave me. I want to go with him," Issy's mother sobbed loudly, straining against the arms of her husband and son.

"You see that tombstone over there," Advocate Berman said, nudging me. He pointed to a dark granite one some twenty feet away. "He was our landlord and he was a real shit. One night my wife and I were at a wedding and she said to me, 'There's your favourite landlord walking in.' I said to her, 'I wish he'd just drop down dead.' About an hour later, while dancing, he actually did drop dead. You can imagine how bad I felt. Every time I come here, I'm reminded of it."

I knew he was trying to distract me from watching the gravediggers widen the hole, but his story made me feel even more anxious.

The coffin was again lowered, this time without any obstruction. The rabbi then took a shovel to the heap of soil piled high at the side of the grave. The clump of earth hit the coffin's wooden lid with a dull thud. The rabbi beckoned other men to come forward and throw a few spadefuls of dark earth into the grave. When it was my turn, I took the spade and scooped the earth, and did the same. The gravediggers finished filling in the grave.

When the service drew to an end, the small group of mourners made their way to Issy's parents and brother, and murmured their condolences.

"I wish you long life," I said, repeating the traditional words of comfort.

I walked back to my car and sat in the driver's seat for a while, unable to move. I had cleaned up the dried blood on the passenger seat and floor—reminders of all that had happened only a few days before. I sat there, overwhelmed by a mixture of emotions. I still could not believe the truth of it, that Issy had taken his own life.

I was also numbed by the realization that in his desperate desire to succeed and not disappoint his parents, he had driven himself to the point of mental collapse. I kept wondering what signs I should have noticed. Whether I could have done anything to help him.

That night I went to Issy's apartment to sit shiva with his family and a few of their friends. His father greeted me with a hug that went on for a while. His pain was palpable.

When I left, his father again hugged me. His mother, her face drained and distraught, whispered the now-familiar question, "Do you know why he did this?" I had no answer that would have given her any comfort.

Many years have passed. As a parent I have experienced my own tragedy and have acquired a greater understanding of Issy's troubled life and anxieties. Yet I still doubt if I could have said anything that would have assuaged the pain of his parents.

NINE

Coffee—A Life Changer

I sat down at my desk to sort more of Sean's papers, but I couldn't concentrate. Leaning back in my chair, I spied a dusty, silver-coloured box on the top shelf of my bookcase. It was coming apart at the corners. I didn't recognize it, but when I took it down, I realized it was our wedding photo album prepared by Anne Fischer, a renowned Cape Town photographer.

I looked at the black-and-white images of Marcia and me about to enter a new phase of our lives. How I appreciated the bonds between us, ever-strengthened over more than five decades, that sustained us now.

Sean relished hearing the story of how Marcia and I met. He would smile broadly and interject wry comments at my slightly embellished tales. He also asked about the lives of our parents and other relatives—what he called "family stories." He would laugh at the quirky tales and grow sombre when I told him about my father's childhood and his fears about family in Europe. His expressions and comments always reflected that he was genuinely fascinated and absorbed. In retrospect, some of my most precious times with Sean were sharing those memories with him.

My idea for our first date was to take Marcia to an exhibition of the Belgian artist James Ensor at the Art Gallery in Cape Town Gardens. My invitation was so unusual that our first date could have been our last. I knew little about Ensor's art; as a student, free admissions were a practical consideration.

I tried to describe to Sean the paintings of Ensor's grotesque masks in bright colours, interspersed with macabre white skeletons, knowing that he was interested and had been attending classes on art therapy.

My choice of venue must have differentiated me from other first dates. I hadn't spirited her away on the customary Saturday afternoon drive to marvel at the stunning sea and mountain vistas of the Cape Peninsula before going for dinner or stopping at some small restaurant for tea and scones, laden with cream and jam. Instead, we walked through a challenging exhibition, delving into the meaning behind the grotesque masks and the spectral figures stripped of flesh, reminding us of the veneers covering the injustices and suffering brought by apartheid South Africa, with its cruel absurdities and oppressive laws.

As I paged through the album, I drifted into a reverie of how our romance had begun with an offhand phone call in December 1963. Elated after passing first-year law school in Cape Town, I needed to share the good news with my mother in Port Elizabeth immediately. I had diligently prepared her for the disappointment of my failing as I tried to balance working full-time in a law office with attending law school.

I dialled the operator to book a long-distance call. She said, "It'll take about an hour. You can make a local call in the meantime. I'll interrupt you when it comes through."

I wondered what to do while waiting. TV hadn't yet been introduced in South Africa. I felt too edgy to read a book or magazine, or listen to the radio, but I had to occupy myself somehow. I took out my small blue diary of phone numbers. I had cut myself off socially due to my unusual study times, but now I felt the need to speak to a friend. I phoned one number after another. No one was home.

My last call was to Frumilla. We had dated about a year before and hadn't seen each other since.

"She's out," said Hillary, her younger sister.

I kept talking, needing contact.

After about ten minutes, Hillary blurted out, "I can't talk any longer. A friend came over and I've been rude. I haven't even made her coffee."

"Why don't you make her coffee? I'll talk to your friend in the meantime." My boldness surprised me. I was on a high. After more than five decades I still remember my words. At the time I could not have guessed the enormous effect my flippant remark would have on my life and on the life of Hillary's friend, Marcia.

Hillary was taken aback by my bravado as much as I was. "Okay, I'll call her."

At this point Sean usually interjected with some exclamation like, "Wow, Dad."

Marcia picked up the phone. She was seventeen, ten years younger than I was, and intrigued, I suppose, by my chutzpah. She was studying chemistry, physics and mathematics. These were my weakest subjects, all way beyond me. After we spoke for fifteen minutes, I knew I wanted to meet her.

"Can I come 'round later and give you a ride home?" I offered.

"That's not a good idea," she said. The conversation hit a low point. "Why don't you come to my house on Saturday afternoon? You can also meet my parents."

I was pleased at her invitation, but being surveyed by parents on a first date seemed so old world, charmingly out of place in 1960s South Africa. I became even more intrigued to meet her.

On Saturday afternoon I parked my red Fiat 1100 in front of her home on Bertha Avenue and apprehensively climbed the front steps. The formality of my visit was reminiscent of the "gentleman caller" in Tennessee Williams's drama *The Glass Menagerie*, set in the American South in the early twentieth century.

I rang the doorbell and retreated to the bottom step. Marcia later described her reaction on seeing me for the first time. "He told me he was tall. Over six foot. I heard the doorbell ring. I opened the door, looked up to see him and there was nothing. Then I looked down, down, down and there he was."

At this point in the story Sean laughed and made some jocular comment like "I didn't know you were ever that short. Did you grow afterwards?"

I laughed and continued with my version of our first meeting.

Marcia welcomed me with a broad smile and opened the door wide. She was dark-haired, with a peaches-and-cream complexion. I appreciated her warmth. So far so good. But I felt uneasy about meeting her parents, Scott and Doreen. I greeted them and was relieved at the absence of probing questions to check if I was a "proper" person to take out their daughter. Doreen spoke with a British accent, which was uncommon in South Africa at the time. Marcia later told me her mother had been an elocution teacher. Scott, wearing a black grease-stained shirt and trousers, smiled and said, "I shouldn't shake your hand now. I've been in the garage repairing a car." He saw my look of surprise and laughed. "Marcia bought a Morris Minor with bursary money she won last year at high school. The body is in great condition, but the car had no engine. I bought spare parts and those that were unavailable I made on my lathe."

I was amazed he could do that. "Is your dad a mechanic?" I later asked Marcia.

"No, he's a chemical engineer but loves working on cars. He's actually the principal of the Maitland Technical College," she explained. "Maybe next time he'll show you his white Jaguar that he fixed up."

She then introduced me to her grandfather, Moss Myers. I had never heard the name Moss before, and assumed it was short for Moses. When he heard I was from Port Elizabeth, he shook my hand warmly. "I lived there for many years and met my wife Anna, Marcia's grandmother, there. Anna passed away a few years ago." He asked me about the school I had attended and where I had lived. He clearly enjoyed reminiscing about his years there. "We should chat more when you come next time," he said, as Marcia gently pulled me away.

In sharp contrast to Scott, Mr. Myers wore an elegant three-piece dark blue suit, a white shirt, tie and gold cufflinks.

"Is he going to a wedding or a funeral?" I asked Marcia.

"No. He always dresses in three-piece suits. It's from the days he owned a large book and stationery store in Port Elizabeth." She added, "He really seems to like you."

As we were about to leave for the art exhibition, she looked at my thin white cotton shirt. "You're not wearing a jersey. It can be cold later. Can I get you one of my father's?" I was amazed—she actually cared about me, a stranger.

"It's okay," I said. "I won't feel the cold." I felt awkward, knowing she was right. I should have brought a jersey. A warm afternoon in Cape Town could turn chilly. Even so, I wasn't prepared to wear her father's, especially on our first date.

At this point Sean usually interjected, "Yes. That is typically Marcia." He called his mom by her first name.

Happily, that date at the Ensor exhibition did not kill our budding relationship. The paintings had a deep relevance to South African reality and gave us much to discuss.

Enough, at least, for her to agree to a second date.

Lennie, one of my friends, liked to quiz me about my dates. After his usual throat-clearing and loud snorting, he asked me whom I had taken out the night before.

"Oh my God. Have you met her father? I did a course at Maitland. He's a tough guy. He has to keep all those thousands of apprentices in check. If anyone's out of line, he takes no crap."

"Are you sure?" Scott seemed mild-mannered and only interested in repairing Marcia's Morris Minor.

He adjusted his thick, horn-rimmed glasses. "I'm positive. He'll eat you for breakfast and not even burp." He laughed at his own description. Then he added, "I'm sure he won't let her marry you. He'll want something better for his daughter."

"Thank you very much," I said. "Actually, they were very nice to me."

"That's how it always starts. But don't be fooled. You have no chance." He laughed.

Sean usually smiled at this part of the story. He adored Scott, remembering him not as a strict college principal but as a doting grandfather.

On our second date, Marcia dropped a bombshell. "I checked up on you. I heard you 'mess girls around.'" I omitted this part in the version of the story I told Sean.

It hadn't occurred to me that having taken out a few women for only one date each had given me such a reputation. I was taken aback. Maybe this was her way of saying she didn't want to see me again.

"Don't tell your father. He'll probably kick me out of the house and warn me to never contact you again." I then told her Lennie's impression of her father.

She laughed, took my hand and said, "You had better behave yourself."

Four hours flew by as we shared our thoughts about the foibles, quirks and idiosyncrasies of our families, our university experiences, and our likes and dislikes. We laughed at our adventures and misadventures and poured out our hopes and aspirations. Marcia spoke about having had a steady boyfriend for the past few years. That relationship had come to an end.

I remembered Mom's words about "settling down." When I met the woman I wanted to marry, my heart would have to be convinced first. But my head would have an equal say in the final decision.

My heart kept sending me signals that I was falling in love. My head felt comfortable about our empathy, common values and dreams. I felt that, based on all of those combined, we could build a lifetime partnership.

I kept thinking, When would be an opportune time to ask her for another date? I recalled her spontaneous concern in offering to lend me her father's jersey to protect me against the chilly night air. Suddenly, I had a flash of intuition.

"You know," I said, "I think we get on so well, we should get married." My spontaneity astonished me.

I waited for her to burst out laughing and say, "You're so funny." I waited for a frown, followed by, "Are you really serious?"

Without a hint of a smile, she said, "Yes. It's a good idea," as if we had been dating for years and she had been waiting for the question.

"When?" I asked, uncertain if she was joking.

"Two years' time. Early in the new year. We'll both have passed our final exams."

I didn't think it appropriate to say it would be an enormous challenge for me to complete my law degree studying part-time by that deadline.

"Of course, you will have to ask my father for his permission," she said with a broad smile. "And that may not be so easy. I'm their only child."

"What if he says no?" I remembered what Lennie had said.

"Well, then it'll be off, or perhaps we'll elope," she laughed. "Who knows what will happen? Grandpa Moss likes you. Maybe he'll put in a good word."

If any of my friends, including Leo, my best friend at school and university, had told me he had set a wedding day on his second date, I would have thought him rash, bordering on ridiculous.

Later that night, alone at my apartment, I was concerned I'd been impetuous. I doubted I could complete all my exams in two years. I remembered Lennie's warnings about Marcia's strict father. Scott might not be too eager to have me as a son-in-law. I feared that my hope of a future together might just be a pipe dream.

Two weeks after meeting Marcia, I returned to Port Elizabeth for the unveiling of my dad's tombstone. Nearly a year had passed since his death. I hoped that the wonderful news of my engagement would lift Mom's spirits. I wanted to tell her face to face, knowing I would be unable to satisfy all her questions and concerns over the phone.

After the ceremony, our friends gathered at Mom's apartment for refreshments. When they left, Mom and I sat in the lounge. She looked tired, her eyes darkened with the resurfacing pain of Dad's death. Now was the time to cheer her up by telling her about my marriage plans.

Mom was taken aback. "Who is Marcia?"

"You will really like her," I said. I showed her a photo and told her how wonderful Marcia was.

Mom pursed her lips, trying to get over her shock. "Who's her family?"

I told her that Marcia's father, Scott, was an engineer, and Doreen was an elocution teacher. Then I lauded her parents and grandfather, even her uncles, aunts and cousins, not daring to admit that I had yet to meet most of them.

Even after more probing questions, I could see that Mom was not convinced, but eventually she said, "I'm sure she's wonderful and I look forward to meeting her."

I hugged Mom.

Three days later, when I had to say goodbye, she said, "You know, you'll have responsibilities and you'll have to pass your exams."

I knew that, and prayed that I could do it.

"We're getting married and I don't even know how to boil an egg." Marcia laughed.

I assured her that having passed my cooking proficiency badge as a Boy Scout, I could show her how.

"I suppose you could also teach me how to open cans of baked beans and corned beef, and light a fire without matches."

The next day I made my way to a bookshop. "Can you recommend a basic cookbook for a young bride?" I asked.

An elderly woman pulled a paperback off a nearby shelf. She handed it to me and walked away.

I glanced at the title: *1001 Ways to Please a Husband: The Bride's Cookbook*. I wondered if it also related to kama sutra—if so, it would be an overwhelming gift for a seventeen-year-old bride to be. I flipped through the pages. It was an introduction to cooking for newlyweds in the form of a diary with narratives interspersed between recipes.

In the years to come, Marcia would love to show it to friends.

"I was thrilled when Henry gave it to me as my first gift. It was then my most prized possession."

When I came to this part, Sean said, "There's no way you could give such a book today to a girlfriend."

But that was in 1964 South Africa, and the title marked a different era. The world has changed, and, fortunately, so have we.

Now we all laugh at the title.

For months, I delayed asking Scott for Marcia's hand in marriage. I didn't expect an outright refusal but feared his saying, "That's nice, but she's young. Why not wait a bit till you know each other better?"

One Saturday afternoon, Marcia urged me finally to ask him. He was working on his white Jaguar. I didn't think it was the best time to approach him, but she was insistent.

"Sorry to disturb you Scott," I said. He crawled out from under the engine in his greasy overalls. I had the feeling he knew what I was going to say. "I would like to marry Marcia. Is it okay?" I asked. My rehearsed speech fell by the wayside.

He smiled and nodded. "Yes, of course." This time he shook my hand, even though his own was covered in oil.

It seemed to me he must have been well prepared for the question by Marcia, Doreen and perhaps also by Grandpa Moss. Scott looked more embarrassed than I felt. From that time on, he and Doreen accepted me as the son they'd never had.

Did we both have our concerns? Yes, we did. There were moments when I thought Marcia might mention that our ten-year age gap could be an impediment. Fortunately, she never did. What she did say one evening was, "I heard that your previous girl friend is beautiful."

"Beauty isn't everything," I said.

On occasion, I would meet Marcia for a quick lunch on the university campus. She'd walk over from the building where she was doing her chemistry practical, arriving in a lab coat stained with burn marks. She wore no makeup. Her hair was slightly dishevelled from mixing, measuring, pouring, and transferring liquids and chemicals in glass vials, watching as the acrid fumes rose up from whatever was boiling in flasks over the Bunsen burners.

One time, Marcia slumped down opposite me. "As I was walking over here, two beautifully dressed women came out of the psychology building. One pointed at me and said, 'That's Marcia, Henry's latest girlfriend.' The other one burst out laughing and said loudly, 'Is that what he's taking out now?'" Marcia looked directly at me. "Was she your former beautiful girlfriend?"

I immediately knew it was. She was studying psychology and was always fashionably dressed. Every Friday afternoon she had her hair done and her nails manicured.

"Yes," I said, "but you get the last laugh."

"Thank you." Marcia smiled, leaned in and kissed my cheek.

The wedding day, set two years earlier on our second date, took place in Cape Town, in the magnificent Gardens Synagogue at the foot of picturesque Table Mountain. The entrance opened onto the greenery and colourful flower beds of the stunning municipal gardens.

Marcia asked Hillary to be her maid of honour. "We're so lucky Frumilla was out that night," Marcia said.

I never saw Frumilla again, although a year later I read that she was part of the thirty-member surgical team at Cape Town's Groote Schuur Hospital, where the first ever human-to-human heart transplant was performed by the South African surgeon, Christiaan Barnard. A twenty-five-year-old woman had been left brain dead following a car accident the day before, and her heart was successfully transplanted into a man. Frumilla died of cancer many years later. I don't know if she was ever aware of how my life and Marcia's had been transformed by a phone call she never received.

The day before the wedding, Marcia and I met with the Chief Rabbi Israel Abrahams, the respected spiritual leader of the congregation, in his study. The rabbi, who was short and portly, stroked his small white beard as he said, "The best advice I can give you as you are about to be married is never to go to sleep at night angry."

In the years to come, whenever one or both of us was upset, we would remind each other of his sage words.

On the following day, I thought about my good fortune.

Here I was, walking down the aisle.

I was awed by the synagogue's impressive interior and the raised, imposing pulpit. And by the sight of Marcia, gorgeous in her white wedding dress.

My speech at the reception included the traditional remarks about absent family. As expected by the guests, I ended with more levity. "You'll recall Queen Elizabeth's visit to South Africa," I began.

She was invited to a junior school, where a seven-year-old girl had been chosen to present her with a bouquet of flowers. In her fluffy pink dress, the girl stumbled on the high steps to the stage. She jumped up, smiled sweetly, and stretched out her small hands to give the flowers to Her Majesty. "I will be careful not to trip when the real Queen arrives," she said.

"Well, for me," I continued, "my real queen has now arrived." I raised my wine glass to Marcia and the guests clapped. Someone said, "Sweet."

That story was appropriate then. Times have changed very much since the 1960s. Now Marcia wouldn't like to be called anybody's queen. I remembered Sean waking up at 6 a.m. in 1997, when we were in Edinburgh, to tell us that Princess Diana had died in a car crash. He had in the past commented on her struggles with mental health issues. He admired Diana immensely because of her empathy for others who were struggling in different ways.

Our best man drove us from the wedding ceremony to the reception in the gleaming white 1950 Jaguar MkVII that Scott had lovingly restored. We were excited at the thought of our honeymoon and starting our married life in Port Elizabeth.

Our other sons also asked how Marcia and I had met and loved to hear the story. They asked, "Did it really happen like that?" I nodded, but I wasn't sure if any of them were convinced. Certainly, no one listened with as much fascination and incredulity as Sean.

If one of our sons told Marcia and me that after two dates he was getting married, I would have thought, *Are you crazy?* Of course, I dared not say that after the example we set.

As I sat in my study, I lingered over the photo of us about to cut the large white wedding cake, bedecked with coloured icing flowers. We stood, our hands cupped over the knife, as if frozen in time. We could not then have dreamt of the highs and lows, the delight and devastation, we would share over the decades.

I gazed at the photo as if mesmerized, conscious of how the commitment to each other and the abiding support of our family have sustained us and furthered our healing as we all faced the sorrow of bereavement.

TEN

Leaving South Africa

One Sunday afternoon Sean flopped down next to me on the couch in our Toronto living room. Twelve years had passed since we'd arrived in Canada. He was now sixteen. Sean looked into my eyes. "Henry. Tell me about South Africa. What was it like when we lived there?" Unlike our other sons, Sean often called me by my first name, instead of "Dad."

I was pleased that he was interested in our previous life. He was nearly four when we left the country, and now the first of our sons to ask about our past.

I have often wondered what effect our conversations about South African history and apartheid had on him and how it shaped his and our other sons' outlook on human rights issues.

I told him about the absurdities and cruelties of apartheid, the injustices suffered by the Blacks and other groups, then called "non-Whites," all under the yoke of the repressive government. I told him about the racist signs, *Slegs Blankes*—Whites Only, plastered on beaches, benches, buses, in parks and swimming pools, on trains and taxi ranks, and in washrooms all over Port Elizabeth. Racial segregation applied to neighbourhoods called townships or locations, schools and universities, cinemas and even burial grounds. It wasn't enough to keep the living apart; apartheid laws dictated the necessity of doing so even in death.

As I spoke, I felt as if I were watching scenes from a movie. The inanities, humiliation, and suffering seemed surreal, and for a moment I wondered how it could all be true. Unfortunately, it was.

"Do you remember Eunice?" I asked.

Sean nodded.

Eunice was a middle-aged Black woman who always had a ready smile, especially for our sons. She worked for us for more than ten years as our cook and housekeeper. The restrictions of apartheid meant there were very limited employment opportunities for her and she had to work as a domestic servant to support her family. To us she was a member of our family. On Sundays I would drive Eunice to the bus terminus where she could take a direct bus home to New Brighton, the large Black township, to visit her family or attend a church meeting. She sat in the back seat of my car to avoid any rumours of breaching the Immorality Act, absurd legislation that prohibited sexual relationships between Whites and Blacks. Maybe I should have worn a driver's uniform or peaked cap. It hardly mattered. I still felt the inanity of the situation.

Apartheid's absurdities abounded.

Sean smiled at my description of the "pencil test." If a person could hold a pencil in their hair when they shook their head, they couldn't be classified as White.

"So if any bald Black person couldn't hold a pencil in their hair, they would automatically be classified as White," he said.

We both laughed uncomfortably.

Arbitrary factors such as skin colour, facial features, and general appearance were all taken into account. At times government decisions were so senseless, members of the same family were classified as belonging to different racial groups with devastating consequences.

The artificiality of such social conventions and the cruelty of the laws had outraged me. It also made me fearful for the future of South Africa.

Sean listened intently. Then he asked, “What happened to my little black poodle when we left?”

I remembered lying next to Sean on his bed a week before we were about to leave our house. He asked, “Is Chico coming with us?”

I had no happy answer. Chico usually slept at the foot of his bed.

I bent my head nearer to Sean. “We will have to give him away. There’s a boy called Piet about five years old, a bit older than you, who always wanted to have a small dog. He promised that he would love Chico and look after him.”

Sean looked at me with pleading eyes. “He’s small. I can hold him on my lap on the airplane.”

“That’s a lovely thought Sean,” I said as I gave him a hug. “Unfortunately, they won’t allow us to do that. I know Piet will look after Chico very well for us.”

Sean pulled the blanket over his face.

Sunday morning, a week later, a van pulled into the driveway. A tall man dressed in khaki and a small boy with closely cropped hair came to our front door. They had come to fetch Chico.

The man told us about their small holding on the outskirts of the city, in Greenbushes. That would be Chico’s new home. His son, Piet, longed for a poodle and Chico would be happy.

“I’m sure you’ll take good care of him,” I said.

Piet nodded and smiled.

I lifted Chico, feeling the anxious throb of his tiny heart. Each of us took turns stroking his small furry head, and saying goodbye. Sean bent over and kissed him. Chico wagged his tail and tried to lick his hands.

As I handed him to Piet, the boy smiled broadly. Sean reached out to take him back, but Piet pulled away.

I put my arms around Sean. "Seanie, Chico has to go to a new home. Piet will look after him nicely." Tears welled up in Sean's eyes.

We all watched the van drive away with Piet holding Chico on his lap, dejection written on the faces of Jonathan, Mark, Kevin and Sean.

What could be worse for a child than parting with a pet?

I told Sean about the eruption of courageous protests in the Black community.

On March 21, 1960, an estimated crowd of 10,000 protested peacefully in the township of Sharpeville. The police opened fire, killing sixty-nine people including eight women and ten children. Many were shot in the back as they fled. That incident was called the Sharpeville Massacre.

I described the Soweto Uprising, a savage police assault on an initially nonviolent student protest in Soweto, a township of Johannesburg. On June 16, 1976, thousands of Black students streamed out of classes carrying placards protesting the 1974 government decree that made Afrikaans—the language of the oppressor—the compulsory language of instruction in Black schools. The death toll from police brutality was estimated at 176. Thousands of schoolchildren were injured. Doctors listed the gunshot wounds as abscesses.

I opened my laptop and searched Google for the jarring photo that had been emblazoned across the front pages of countless newspapers—a man carrying the limp body of twelve-year-old Hector Pieterson after he had been shot by the police. Sean looked and listened with rapt attention, relating to students close in age to him, horrified by the brutality.

As I have come to understand more of his thoughts, I believe that having been born in South Africa made him acutely aware of issues of justice and fairness in society for all people.

Then I shared something else with him: our anxieties.

Had we remained in South Africa, Jonathan would have been the first of our sons required to report for army duty. In due course, the Defence Force would have conscripted Mark, Kevin and Sean as well. As I spoke in the quiet of my Canadian living room, I pictured my four sons crammed inside an army vehicle, fingers on a trigger, waiting to be ordered to open fire on Black South Africans. All this bolstered the apartheid system.

Sean looked surprised. "Do you really mean that if we stayed we could have been ordered to fire bullets on Black schoolchildren?"

I nodded. When we left South Africa, Jonathan was already twelve years old, Mark ten, Kevin six and Sean four.

"Yes. Jonathan would have been called up into the army within five years."

After describing the horrors of apartheid, I was happy to tell Sean about the amusing incidents that occurred as we left our house at 37 Short Road.

Jonathan had called out, "Let's look at our names." Together, we walked down the long driveway that wound through an avenue of trees. Jonathan, Mark and Kevin had scratched their names in the wet cement when the driveway was built. The three of them found their names right away. They had left their mark.

"Where's my name?" Sean asked, his lip trembling.

"Seanie, you weren't born yet when we built the driveway," I said. "So we couldn't scratch your name on it."

Only one thing could console him. A red popsicle.

He smiled as I told him the story. "Yes, and you still didn't scratch my name on afterwards."

"But Sean, you were a great helper." He had insisted on carrying boxes nearly half his height to the Afrovan truck for shipment to Canada.

Our sons had brought Marcia and me their favourite clothes, Meccano sets, books, Snakes and Ladders, checker and chess sets to pack. Their faces crumpled when Marcia shook her head. "We can't take all that with us. There's no room."

Sean handed us handfuls of soft toys, and we melted. "Okay, but remember, we can't take everything with us."

There were our prepared lists that we tried to follow.

We had a deadline to complete our tasks. Scott and Doreen had emigrated ahead of us in anticipation of our leaving. Soon after their arrival in Canada, Doreen was diagnosed with ovarian cancer. Marcia flew over to be at her mother's bedside in her final moments. In an act of selflessness and courage, Doreen had hidden her symptoms in South Africa. She had avoided going to a doctor until she arrived in Canada, afraid that her illness would delay their immigration, and ours.

Scott insisted on remaining in Toronto. Months later when we called to tell him that we had received our acceptance, he flew back to help us declutter and pack up.

Sean, many years later, would diligently and thoughtfully attend to his own preparations. He sorted his files, his notebooks, medical records, musical tapes, discs and photos. He carefully chose the time and method of his death.

As I spoke to Sean that Sunday afternoon, I thought back to the seven of us, including Scott, climbing the passenger stairs into the airplane from the tarmac of the Port Elizabeth airport. Each of us carried the maximum the airline would allow. Kevin's and Sean's backpacks bulged with teddy bears and soft toys.

Kevin and Sean wriggled in their seats, excited to be embarking on a great adventure. Jonathan and Mark realized that they were leaving all their friends behind and might never see them again.

We were leaving.

We had somehow managed to meet the three-month deadline to take up our landed immigrant status. The near-impossible timeline meant that I would have to return to South Africa in just four weeks to finalize the sale of my real estate interests.

I closed my eyes and held Marcia's hand. A throb of exhilaration washed over me—a new beginning. Yet uncertainty gnawed at me. Apartheid's race laws still endured and continued to take a toll on the majority of South Africans. We didn't envision that democratic elections would take place slightly more than a decade later.

We were leaving wonderful friends, family, employees, professional and business associates, and so many more, not knowing when, if ever, we would meet again.

There would be the wrenching loss of the familiar that leaving the country of one's birth entails: our home, South Africa's breathtaking scenery, the white sandy beaches with crashing waves, the streets, stores and restaurants that we frequented, and so much more. Interwoven with loss was anxiety about the challenges we would face in our adopted country: finding a home and schools for our sons, requalifying as a lawyer, obtaining employment and financially supporting our family of six.

When I'd arrived in Port Elizabeth at age ten everything was strange: the school, teachers, streets, stores, people, buses and buildings. It would be the same for our sons. The difference was, they had each other.

I thought about the countless people around the world forced to flee as refugees, travelling in leaky boats or trudging over searing deserts and rugged mountain paths. Others, bound tightly to family or debt, or lacking the criteria for entering another country, have no choice but to remain subject to invisible walls of racial or religious prejudice.

I felt a wave of sadness as I thought of Dad's parents, brothers, sister, aunts and family in Latvia. Unable to leave, they had been brutally murdered by the Nazi invaders and their eager accomplices during World War II.

Our first four weeks in Toronto were hectic. We rented a townhouse at York Mills and Bayview Avenue, purchased a second-hand Chevy Impala, and enrolled our sons in schools. We were all excited to be living in a large metropolis. Simply strolling the wide aisles of supermarkets, with their enormous array of products, was for us a mind-boggling experience.

Marcia pointed to the walk-in closet adjoining our bedroom. "See, your clothes are all there, waiting for your return."

Within a few short weeks, I was again heading for the airport. I hugged everyone goodbye. "When are you coming back?" Sean asked. Soon, I told him, and hoped that it was true. I did not expect that it would take nearly a year to finalize the sale of my South African real estate.

Each day I called Marcia from Port Elizabeth and felt the pain of being an absentee husband and father. She shared the difficulties she faced as a "single parent," relaying in one phone call what Sean had said when his teacher asked about her pupils' families. "I have a mother, a grandfather, and will have a father one day soon." He'd conveniently erased his older brothers in one fell swoop. I saw Sean's cute, smiling face before me. I desperately wanted to be a real father as soon as possible.

Six months after I returned to Canada, my first Canadian winter arrived. In heavy snow Sean built an igloo. I applauded his sturdy structure, knowing we would all face many challenges in building our own lives in our new home.

ELEVEN

Germs of Anxiety

I sat in my armchair and reflected on Sean's many consuming anxieties. I believed I would never fathom the exact cause of his being drawn into darkness. Yet I wondered if growing up in a house filled with turbulence and challenges faced by the family could have led him to feel unsettled.

One morning in 1990, after we had been in Canada for ten years, I heard Sean shout from the family room, "Come and look. Jonathan is being arrested!"

Marcia and I rushed to the television as Sean pointed to the screen calling out, "Look. Look!"

The three of us watched in shock as Jonathan was dragged along the ground and pushed into a police van.

Sean, then fourteen, looked at me with puckered brow. "Do you think Jonathan will go to jail?"

"I hope not," although what we saw on television seemed to contradict my words.

Sean looked stunned as he continued to fixate on the TV screen. Of all our four sons, he was closest to Jonathan; he was the little kid brother that Jonathan wanted to look after. They had gone canoeing together, shared their love of music, and even lived together downtown for a while.

Like the rest of the country, we had been following media coverage of the Oka uprising. Mohawks living on the reserve of Kanesatake in Quebec had blocked a road leading to a golf course in the town of Oka and ignored a court injunction to stand down. Town officials had foolishly voted to build condominiums and expand the golf course into a forest called "The Pines" that included a burial ground the Mohawks had long claimed as their own. The standoff made international headlines that raised awareness of Indigenous issues, especially those related to land claims.

Jonathan had joined the "Peace Camp" in support of the Mohawks. An estimated 10,000 people gathered on the outskirts of the town of Oka, as near The Pines as the Sûreté du Québec, the provincial police, would allow.

Before Jonathan left, Sean quizzed him. "What will you do there? Is it safe?"

"I don't know," he answered, and pursed his lips for a few seconds. "But I have to show solidarity. I'm sure you understand. It's wrong what's happening. We've often spoken with Dad about what's right and fair, especially coming from South Africa."

Sean nodded. Apparently, all our discussions about apartheid and social justice had resonated with our oldest son and Sean.

From the moment Jonathan left Toronto, Sean was riveted to each newscast on the Oka crisis. Marcia and I were proud that Jonathan cared enough to take a stand. We were also concerned for his safety at the Peace Camp.

Sean quizzed me daily. "Do you think Jonathan will be okay?" I assured him that all would be fine—not that I knew. I sensed he wasn't convinced by my reply.

On July 11 we watched TV coverage of the Sûreté du Québec, in riot gear with guns blazing, storming the blockade at Kanesatake. After fifteen minutes of mayhem, the police retreated, but not before a thirty-one-year-old officer, Marcel Lemay, had been tragically killed in an exchange of gunfire. Two thousand police were sent to Oka on the heels of the attack. They were later replaced by 4,500 Canadian soldiers with tanks and formidable military equipment for land and air support. All this weaponry and personnel were positioned against thousands of civilians protesting the abysmal disregard of Indigenous rights.

Marcia and I were horrified, watching the police and the military mobilization. Hadn't we left all this behind us in South Africa?

The Peace Camp was ringed with barbed wire and tightly guarded. As the standoff continued, protesters were allowed to leave, but no one could enter. What started as thousands in the Peace Camp began to dwindle rapidly. We wondered if Jonathan would leave as well.

Eventually, he phoned to tell us that he and nine others were remaining. Everyone else had left. Again, I admired their stand but was anxious for their welfare.

The scene of Jonathan being dragged into that police van was as horrific for us as it would have been for any parent. For me the shock was alleviated by some understanding of the court process. There would be a bail hearing and later a trial that should, hopefully, lead to a just end. But for Marcia and Sean the shock was deeper and more enduring. My legalistic explanations did not appear to give them much comfort.

Thankfully, Jonathan called us later that day. "The ten of us have been charged with obstructing the police. We're going to fight the case. We're not guilty. The police obstructed us. We're hiring a Quebec lawyer."

Sean asked me, "Are you going there to defend them?"

I explained that I wasn't licensed to practice in Quebec. I could, however, assist. I called the lawyer representing the group, concerned about whether he'd be able to obtain an acquittal.

I listened closely as he spoke in a rich Quebecois accent. "I've handled many cases like this, and I put up a strong defence."

"But did you ever get a not-guilty verdict?"

"No. Not really. It's not easy, but we make our point and get a lot of press coverage."

That's not what I wanted to hear. A criminal conviction had serious long-term consequences. Jonathan and the other nine accused were adamant. If their sentence included a fine, Jonathan said they would refuse to pay it. They were determined to go to jail as a matter of principle.

"Maybe it's better to pay the fine," Sean said. He appeared dismayed that they would rather go to jail.

With the permission of all the accused, I joined the defence team with my law partner, Ron Segal. Originally from Montreal, Ron guided me through the Quebec legal system.

The trial started with the prosecutor apologizing to the judge—the police witnesses had been given the wrong date for the trial. The judge frowned. "I will proceed with the trial and split the charges," the prosecutor said.

"What does he mean?" I whispered to Ron.

He explained that the prosecutor would obtain his proof by calling the accused to give evidence against each other.

I was aghast at the procedure. Not being a criminal lawyer, I had not heard of this concept. "This is third-world justice," I muttered softly.

The judge and prosecutor heard my comment and glared at me. For a moment I thought I would be charged with contempt of court.

The judge rose as if in a huff. "The court will take a short recess." He hastened out, black gown billowing behind him.

The prosecutor's face reddened. Saliva sprayed onto my jacket as he said, "If you do that again I will ask the judge to exclude you from the court."

I realized I had not been smart.

"I apologize, Your Honour," I said when the judge returned, "but I've never heard of such a procedure before." I found out later that splitting the charges was indeed part of the law.

Jonathan and the other accused had no problem with the prosecutor's plan. They were happy to tell the court why they wouldn't leave the Peace Camp.

I was surprised that they agreed and anxious how it would affect the outcome of the trial.

Jonathan was called to the witness box and sworn in. Clearly, he had taken steps to present himself in the best possible light. At the time of his arrest, he was unshaven, with long, unruly hair and grungy clothes. In court, he appeared as a short-haired, clean-shaven, University of Toronto criminology student in a dark blue blazer, white shirt and tie.

He told the judge that he joined the Peace Camp to support the Mohawks. He wanted to help create awareness of the injustice meted out to the Canadian Indigenous people. He denied that he and the other nine accused had obstructed the police as the prosecutor claimed.

The next accused called as a witness was a grandmother and retired school teacher from British Columbia. She said that she had watched the crisis unfold on television and was distressed by all the violence. The death of the police officer horrified her. She wanted to "do something" to help defuse the situation, and so she drove across Canada in her motorhome to join the Peace Camp.

The judge sat behind his bench writing notes. From time to time he glanced at the various witnesses giving evidence. Suddenly, he put down his pen and scowled at the prosecutor. "Are you going on with your case?" he asked.

"No, Your Honour," the prosecutor said quickly. He withdrew the charges against the accused.

The case was over.

The judge nodded. "It seems to me that instead of the accused obstructing the police, the police obstructed them while they were peacefully there." He closed his notebook and strode out of the court.

I called home to relate the good news, and Sean answered. Marcia told me later that he had waited near the phone all day to hear the court's decision.

"Wow, that's fantastic," Sean said. "We're so proud of Jonathan for standing up for his principles."

Although I admired Jonathan's ethical stance and was relieved at the outcome, Marcia and I seemingly aged years in the process!

Sean had been stressed since Jonathan's arrest. I was happy to hear the relief in his voice.

On the morning of March 1, 1990, we were watching news coverage of a hotel fire in Cairo. As flames spewed out of the six-storey, 630-room Heliopolis Sheraton, Sean, the avid TV watcher of the family, looked at me anxiously. "I hope Mark and Scott aren't in that hotel." Mark, our second son, had been studying in Israel and his grandfather, Scott, had arranged to take him to Egypt for a short vacation.

I assured him it was very unlikely they would be in that particular hotel on that night.

"But you can't really be sure. Can you?" Sean said.

"I can't be absolutely sure. But you have to be positive, Sean. Don't always look on the down side." I waited for his reply. He remained silent.

All of us in the house, but particularly Sean, watched the television constantly to see what would unfold. Seventeen people died in the fire that day. Another seventy were injured, many of them suffering broken bones, jumping out of windows or sliding down bedsheets, desperate to escape the inferno. The blaze had been ignited by sparks from a clay oven in a Nubian tent restaurant next door that featured belly dancing. A strong wind stoked the fire and swept it into the hotel, which lacked both fire alarms and sprinkler systems.

The phone rang. It was Mark, in Cairo. "Grandpa and I were in the Sheraton. You must have seen it on television. Close to midnight Grandpa woke me saying there was a bright light coming into the bedroom. I got up, looked outside and saw a fire. I told him to grab his passport and pushed him out of the door. We ran down the stairs and outside in our pyjamas."

"Are you and Scott okay?" I called out.

"We're fine. Lots of people died," Mark said. "Our room was completely burnt out. We're lucky to be alive."

Scott came to the phone. "Mark's quick action saved our lives. I was standing there looking out of the window. He grabbed my arm and pushed me out of the room. We left everything behind."

Marcia and I were stunned. Sean looked at me and said, "So who was right about the hotel?"

Two days later Scott returned to Canada, and Mark to Israel.

The airport in Toronto was teeming with photographers and TV cameras, to meet Scott. He came out carrying a flimsy plastic shopping bag with Arabic lettering. The bag contained the pyjamas he'd been wearing when he rushed out of the hotel. As reporters interviewed him, he smiled. He seemed bemused by the welcome.

Sean pointed to Scott's feet. "Wow, Grampy. Look at your yellow shoes."

Scott laughed, saying he'd bought them at a bazaar in Cairo.

I never saw him wear those shoes again.

"Did you and Mark watch the belly dancers the night before the fire?" I asked. Sean grinned, intrigued at the thought.

Scott laughed. "No," he said, "we missed that. I was embarrassed walking with the Canadian Consul through the streets of Cairo in my pyjamas 'til I noticed nobody was looking at me. They were all wearing similar outfits." Then he added, "We were lucky. I feel so sorry for those who didn't get out in time."

The first years of building up the law practice meant coming home late at night. On the rare occasions that I came home early, Sean asked, "Henry, what was your day like?"

I couldn't fob him off with a quick, "It was fine." He sat next to me and waited for a full answer. I felt a warm glow; he cared.

His reaching out to me filled me with joy. How I wished, like so many parents, that I had spent more time with my children.

Sean often complained that as the youngest child he hadn't gotten as much attention as his siblings. He pointed to all the photos and videos of the others as toddlers. By contrast, there were few of him.

Treasured moments flashed before me. How his eyes focused on my face as I answered questions. He asked about everything, from our life in South Africa, our family history, to what I did during the day.

I thought of the many places Marcia and I had visited, often joined by one or more of our sons: South Africa, England, Mexico, Europe, Egypt, Israel, the United States. There were cruises around the Caribbean and canoe trips in northern Ontario. There were the moments of fun before we emigrated from the city of their birth: visiting Port Elizabeth's parks and gorgeous beaches, driving along the coast, scampering on rocks, wading in pools, spending time with friends, riding horses on our farm, going to the museum and the aquarium. Then in Toronto, more enrichment: the Science Centre, the Zoo, the Art Gallery of Ontario, Ontario Place, and the Royal Ontario Museum. But of all we had done together as a family, I cherished most the rare, quiet times—the moments we listened to our sons' hopes and fears, trying to fathom the challenges each one faced.

As our sons grow older, memories of the fun occasions we shared with them as children slowly fade, like faces in cracked black-and-white family photographs. The time not spent together becomes a lingering regret.

Sean, the last of our sons to leave home, grew increasingly anxious about all that swirled around the house. Whether it was Jonathan's arrest at Oka, or Scott and Mark surviving the disastrous fire in Cairo, he worried about everyone.

Marcia and I, however, worried about him.

His outbursts began in his early twenties and continued for a few years. He was still living with us. He would come into our bedroom at eleven o'clock at night. Just as we were about to go to sleep, he'd say, "Can I ask you a quick question?" I agreed. What was supposed to take a few minutes became an hour or two discussion that ranged over various concerns: career choices, his relationship with his psychiatrist and his physiotherapist, whether or not he should accept a social invitation.

Well past midnight, I said that I had to put off the lights. The alarm was going off at six.

"I'm nearly finished." But he continued vacillating over the same issues. At times he appeared to agree with my suggested solutions, but later he raised the identical concerns. Nothing Marcia and I could say seemed to lead to a resolution. He would overthink each problem, and his indecision gnawed at him.

Eventually I said, "Sean, try to keep it simple. Don't analyze everything to death." In retrospect I should have used a different word.

He nodded and thanked me for my advice but continued the discussion.

"Sean, it's one o'clock. I must go to sleep. You sleep 'til eleven in the morning. I can't."

"It's not my fault I can't fall asleep," he shouted. "You're being very unreasonable not talking to me."

He stomped out of our bedroom, slammed the door behind him, and banged the passage wall with his fist.

The first few times that happened, I was shocked. I didn't know how to react. Thereafter I engaged him in conversation earlier in the evening. By ten o'clock the discussion came to an end, even though he hadn't accepted much of my or Marcia's opinions.

After his first outburst, Marcia and I tried to ensure that he saw his psychiatrist regularly, reminded him to take his meds as prescribed, urged him to make social arrangements whether through yoga, meditation classes, or elsewhere. We often invited him to accompany us on walks, visits to our cottage, restaurants, cinema or theatre. For a while he accepted many of our invitations.

Later, he declined most of them.

One morning, in the final year of writing her doctoral thesis at York University in Toronto, Marcia burst into my study. "I just got an email from the Open University in England. I've been offered a research fellowship for a year! It's amazing." She paused. "Obviously, I can't take it."

"You cannot not go," I said—a double negative, meaning yes. This didn't show excessive excitement on my part, but suggested strongly that she shouldn't refuse. It was an incredible opportunity for her.

I was proud of Marcia receiving the offer. A year was a long time. But we would manage somehow.

Her studies started a fascinating journey for our whole family. In South Africa, at the age of nineteen, Marcia had completed a Bachelor of Science in math, chemistry and physics. She had a lingering awareness that she had never studied the arts, and so when all the boys were at school in Toronto, she completed her Masters and PhD at York University, focusing on drama. This began a long love affair with the theatre that led to her doing a postdoctoral fellowship in England and becoming a tenured associate professor at York University.

Sean once asked her what it had been like to go back to university as a mature student.

Marcia told him about going to the library and taking a book on Mandela from the stacks. "I quickly looked over my shoulder to see if anyone was watching and would report me to the secret police. Then I realized I was in Canada, not South Africa, and the secret police weren't watching me," she said, smiling. "Old habits take time to die."

I couldn't have imagined when we married how, through her passion for theatre, our world would open up to new issues and ideas that instilled in our children a deep interest in social justice and human rights.

Our friends' reactions to Marcia's leaving for London were mixed. Most of them congratulated her warmly. I was outraged when one whispered to me, "I wouldn't let my wife go to London for a year!"

One of our acquaintances, Brian, tactlessly asked me one day, "Will she come back?"

"Of course," I said without any hesitation.

Later that night, Sean came into my study and closed the door behind him. "I heard what Brian said. Do you think there's a chance Mom won't come back?"

"I'm sure she will," I said. I believed that to be so, but life provides no guarantees.

Her absence would be more difficult for Sean. Through her he had not only developed an avid interest in theatre; he also talked with her for hours about his health concerns and treatment options. These conversations would continue in emails and phone calls to London.

During her year away, Sean was the only one of our four sons still living at home. I tried to spend as much time with him as possible. Often he declined my offers to go out to restaurants or elsewhere, saying he was tired.

I flew to London every month to join Marcia in the small apartment she had rented in Pimlico. All our sons visited her as well, which gave her quality time with each of them.

Scott went to visit Marcia on May 15. They arranged to fly back together on Sunday, May 26, in time for Marcia to face her PhD defence on Tuesday. Sadly, they didn't travel back together.

Whenever Scott was in London he always contacted his cousins, John and Lorna. He and John decided to travel to Ireland. There he contracted food poisoning. He consulted a doctor who gave him medication and advised him to stop taking his blood thinner medication. The two immediately returned to London.

Late at night on Wednesday, May 23, Scott suffered a massive heart attack. Marcia frantically searched the phone directory for the emergency number. An ambulance arrived within fifteen minutes, and she accompanied him to St. Thomas Hospital.

She called me from the hospital, distraught.

"I'll take the first flight over," I said.

Later that night Marcia called again. "The cardiologist thinks he may not survive. If he does, he won't have quality of life. They want to know if they should keep him on life support. What do you think?" Could there be a more difficult decision?

"While there is life there is hope." In my shock I could only offer a cliché. I couldn't bear being part of the decision to end his life no matter how tenuous it was—Scott meant so much to me.

"He wouldn't want to live in a vegetative state," Marcia said.

I booked the earliest morning flight. Sean helped me pack and stayed up until the taxi arrived. "I hope Grampy pulls through," he said. His face was pale, his eyes downcast. I couldn't tell him that Scott might not recover. There was a special bond between them. Scott lived in a townhouse five minutes away by car, and every night he came to our house for supper. Sean would ask Scott how he was doing, and there would be laughter and teasing. Sean adored him.

From Heathrow Airport I went directly to St. Thomas Hospital. Marcia, Jonathan, Kevin and Alisa were gathered in the waiting area. Kevin and Alisa had been in France, having recently stayed with Marcia. Jonathan was visiting.

A nurse led me into the intensive care unit. I moved slowly to Scott's bedside. He was in a coma, deeply drugged, attached to tubes and beeping monitors. We took turns reading or talking to him. We were told that hearing is the last sense to go.

On the evening of Friday, May 24, he passed away. He was seventy-nine. We never had to make the decision about disconnecting him from life support.

Marcia called Sean and Mark in Toronto. They were both devastated. They loved him so much.

John tried to obtain authorizations over the weekend for Scott's body to be flown to Toronto, but government departments were operating only on voicemail. He assured us he would succeed at the latest by Monday. In Toronto Mark and Lisa made all the arrangements for the funeral, tentatively planned for Thursday.

On Sunday, in Scott's place, I flew back to Toronto with Marcia. As we buckled our seatbelts Marcia said, "I feel terrible leaving Dad behind. His last words to me as we rode in the ambulance were, 'I'm so sorry I disturbed your work.'" Then she added, "I'm in a state of shock, but I must proceed with the defence for his sake."

On Wednesday, May 29, the afternoon before the internment, we visited Benjamin's Park Memorial Chapel. Marcia had asked to see Scott for the last time. He was covered in a white shroud. She approached his ashen face and whispered, "Dad, I want you to know …" And in a broken voice continued, "Yesterday I passed my defence. Thank you for all your inspiration and encouragement. Always."

Scott was laid to rest at the Dawes Road Cemetery beside his beloved wife, Doreen.

Our four sons were all pallbearers to honour their beloved grandfather.

Travelling was not easy for Sean. But he did visit Marcia. One evening she returned from the university and found the apartment lock sprung from the inside. She knocked and asked Sean to open the door. No answer. She kept knocked and calling. Eventually, Sean yelled, "Leave me alone. I'm not opening the door."

Frantic, she called me and asked what to do. She had phoned him many times but he wouldn't respond. I was very concerned. I wished I had a magical incantation like Aladdin's "Open Sesame" that would make the door slide open.

After many unanswered calls and emails from me, Sean

eventually answered the phone. "Yes. What do you want?" I asked him to unlatch the lock. He put down the phone. After more agitated calls from Toronto, I threatened, as a last resort, to call the police. He then complied. Later he apologized profusely saying that he had had a panic attack.

All families have their unique predicaments. It is not always the severity of the challenges they face but the response to them that matters most. Each member of our family became aware that Sean needed help as he continued to vigorously wrestle his personal demons.

TWELVE

Ships Passing in the Night

Twenty-six years had passed since we all arrived in Canada in 1980, and our family had grown. Jonathan had married Pam, Mark married Lisa and Kevin, Alisa. Sean remained single, revelling in his new-found status as an uncle. He happily related to Marcia and me the details of every interaction he had with his three nephews.

One afternoon Jonathan invited the three of us over. As we stepped through the door, he couldn't contain his excitement. "Pam's expecting a little girl!"

Marcia and I hugged them both with repeated mazeltovs.

Sean stood to the side, grinning. "Congratulations. The way things were going I thought I would only have nephews." He laughed. "Now I'll have a niece as well."

But our hopes did not go as anticipated.

I had booked a flight to Latvia to attend the unveiling of the Memorial Wall in Liepaja. This monument listed the names of the 6,422 men, women and children—including my Blumberg grandparents, uncles, aunts and cousins—murdered by the Nazis and their willing Latvian accomplices. I agonized over whether to go, as the unveiling was close to Pam's due date.

Pam assured me. "It's okay. You should go. Nothing will happen in the next few days." I realized later that my daughter-in-law must have known otherwise.

Sean offered to drive me to the airport. "On the way, you can tell me more about why you're going to Latvia," he said.

I told him about the "Holocaust by Bullets." The Jewish citizens of Liepaja were murdered at different sites in the city and also lined up at the side of trenches dug deep into the white sea sand on the beach at Skede, and shot.

"Do we still have family left there?" Sean asked. He seemed genuinely interested.

I told him about my cousin Bella and her daughter, Rita, who were the sole surviving members of the Blumberg family living in Latvia. I had located them after many years of delving through archival records and websites.

The night before the unveiling, I received the joyous call from Marcia, telling me of the birth of our granddaughter, weighing 6 lb. 1 oz, born on a Sunday afternoon at 4:45 p.m. I smiled at these precise details, as if one ounce or one minute could make a difference.

I was pleased to hear that Jonathan and Pam had chosen the name Sasha Bella in memory of Marcia's and my grandmothers, Sarah Sacks and Sarah Altshuler. The baby's second name, Bella, was in memory of Pam's father, Bruce Stein. The name Bella further resonated with me, having reconnected with my cousin.

The birth of Sasha Bella was more than just a wonderfully uplifting moment for me and my immediate family. Here I was, receiving this news in a place steeped in sadness. It seemed a miracle, on the eve of commemorating our painful past, to welcome a new addition to the remaining Blumberg family. The cycle of life continued.

The night after the ceremony in Liepaja the incessant ringing of my cell phone woke me. I fumbled in the dark to find it. Who would call me in the middle of the night?

"Are you awake?" Marcia asked. Her voice was halting.

I immediately sensed that something was terribly wrong.

"We're worried about Sasha. Things aren't right. Pam was holding her and the baby had difficulty breathing. They gave her oxygen and rushed her over to SickKids ICU. They're doing tests, but don't know anything yet. It may take a while 'till we know."

The next day, on my flight home from Riga to Toronto, my mind was filled with angst. My thoughts flitted from the sombre unveiling of the monument to the joyous birth of Sasha Bella, to fear of what the tests would show. I yearned to be with my family; I wanted us all to be together.

During the weeks that followed Marcia and I waited anxiously for each test result. Sean, who was still living at home, asked daily, "Have you heard anything more?"

Eventually, the medical team had answers. They confirmed that Sasha had been born with a liver disease, Alagille Syndrome, and a severe heart condition called pulmonary atresia. She faced incredible challenges, including multiple catheterizations and heart surgeries.

We prayed that things would turn out well. With every successful treatment, our hopes soared.

Still, over the next year, her long-term future grew uncertain. We then realized that every moment, every experience with her, was precious. Marcia and I and at times Sean visited her on a near daily basis at their house and at SickKids Hospital. We were amazed at her long fingers that could turn fragile pages in a telephone book without tearing them. We marvelled at her love of potato crisps, crushed ice, watermelon toothpaste, the way she danced in her crib to Stevie Wonder. We delighted at the big grin she always had for her parents, and for Marcia, Sean and me. We laughed when she'd slap her forehead as if to say, "Oy vey."

She shone at her first birthday party, fascinated by the one lit candle on the chocolate cake. Smiling mischievously, she scooped out cake with her long fingers and quickly stuffed it into her mouth, gurgling with glee at our circle of smiles.

Sam, their family's beloved dog, looked up with pleading eyes. Tongue hanging out, he begged for cake to be thrown his way.

She watched Pam open all the presents and cards. Giggling with delight, Sasha examined a gift for a moment and stretched out her arms, eager for the next present. Sean stood beaming, absorbed in her obvious enjoyment of the moment.

At eighteen months, in December 2005, she suffered severe complications after another heart surgery. By this time, Jonathan and Pam had been living at SickKids Hospital for five months, with Pam there during the day and Jonathan sleeping over each night. Marcia and I visited almost daily. Often Sean accompanied us and happily played with her, but when we left the broad smile that he had had for her faded.

We marvelled at Sasha's zest for life.

No matter what she was facing, there she was, that beautiful blonde, curly-haired child with the big welcoming smile.

With each new intervention and procedure, the doctors and nurses worked hard to improve her condition. But after several months, it became clear that their options were limited. Sasha survived her last surgery, but her liver could not handle the enormous stress.

Marcia and I were heartbroken, watching her fight to survive, knowing that little more could be done. Sean seldom smiled and retreated to his room after dinner. We ourselves were powerless to do more than provide as much love as possible for our children and our grandchild.

Jonathan and Pam now faced one of the hardest decisions a parent ever has to make. "We have to bring her home to be with everything she loves and try to give her some quality of life," Jonathan said.

Pam slowly nodded.

Sasha had been at SickKid's for what seemed an eternity. Jonathan and Pam contacted the Temmy Latner Centre, where the Dr. Jay Children's Grief Program is based. They offer parents the emotional support needed to take a dying child home, or to stay in the hospital if that is their choice. Their mission is to help the whole family grieve, remember and honour their child.

As Jonathan told us one night, "The hospital can't do much more. We have to face the reality of her death."

There were no more procedures.

It was time to bring her home.

For her to return home meant the end was near. Her care team expected her to live for only a few days. For the nurses who had cared for her for many months, it was a trying time. Several wrote cards, expressing warm and loving thoughts. Their hugs and words became part of our own comforting, cherished memories. Her nurse Julie wrote,

> Dearest Sasha, my favourite memory of you is your big toothy smile with round chubby cheeks and eyes brighter than stars. Your "Hi's!" would make my heart happy to see you so happy heading out in your pram for a promenade that would light up the ward. You will always have a special place in my heart for all that I have learned from you in your too-short time here. Thank you for this gift. — Julie A.

Sasha's cardiologist, Dr. Jennifer Russell, said, "She was a bright, happy little girl. She loved an audience. I'd come by with a big medical team and she would ham it up. She'd babble away at us: 'Hi, Hi, Hi.'"

Sasha smiled when she saw the family car for the first time in five months. As they drove home, Jonathan watched her in her car seat, staring intently out the window, quietly humming to herself. At home Sam greeted her with tail wagging. As Pam carried her around, showing her the familiar rooms and toys, Sasha's eyes widened with recognition. That evening, she giggled and splashed in the bath.

"She slept with us in our own bed for the first night." Jonathan was smiling as he told us the next day. "We played and sang songs together. It was an incredible milestone for us."

At home she was her happiest, we could all see that. There she was surrounded by the warmth of family and the familiar joys and pleasures she so loved.

Pam rubbed Sasha's little hand on her stomach and told her that she was going to have a baby sister soon. Jonathan told me, "I don't know if she understood but she smiled anyway as she stroked Pam's tummy."

To everyone's surprise, her final days turned into weeks.

Her second birthday was a treasured event celebrated with the family: Pam's mother, Lorna Stein, siblings Kenny, Rayna and Jessica with their spouses and children, and Marcia and I with our sons, their spouses and children. We savoured the many bittersweet, poignant moments, knowing that this June 6, five weeks after she'd returned from hospital, would be Sasha's last birthday with us all.

Everyone wanted to make each moment as meaningful as possible for Sasha.

Marcia, Sean and I climbed the stairs to Pam and Jonathan's house with festive balloons in pink, blue and yellow.

The aroma of barbecue wafted into the house. Sam strained at Jonathan's feet, lusting after morsels. Sasha, in a pink jacket, was sucking on a white pacifier, her light blonde hair bobbing in a little ponytail on her crown.

She gave her wide smile as the big birthday cake with two candles was set down before her. She stuck her fork into the cake. I couldn't keep my eyes off Jonathan, singing her birthday song with tears rolling down his face.

She played a game of taking turns, sucking on a lollipop then handing it to Jonathan to lick. At one point she handed the lollipop to Sean, and while we laughed as he licked it, I noticed his downcast eyes. Playfully, she passed the lollipop around before giving it to Jonathan to lick again.

She smiled as she tried to bounce the birthday balloon bouquet sent by the palliative care team.

Jonathan gave Sasha her medicine, and Pam started opening the gifts. Soon, her tiredness cut the party short.

As the end approached, Jonathan and Pam accepted a photo session offered by Now I Lay Me Down to Sleep, a group of professional photographers who create tender sessions for palliative care children and their families.

Later, when I looked at the black-and-white photos, I thought of Pam and Jonathan's heart-wrenching emotions as they held Sasha for these final images. They knew these photos would be among the last mementoes of their treasured memories of her life and the short time they spent together.

Two weeks after her second birthday, on the afternoon of June 20, 2006, I sat next to Sasha on Jonathan and Pam's bed, touching her small hand. Marcia sat on the other side, gently stroking her arm. Marcia, Jonathan and I sang "Baa Baa Black Sheep" and touched her brow.

Her breathing slowed and grew irregular.

Quietly, at 6:20 p.m. that night, she left us. She was twenty-four months old.

Our beloved Sasha had fought the brave fight and lived her short life to the fullest.

Jonathan and Pam dressed her in a beautiful pink dress and lay with her until the undertakers came.

My chest tightened as I watched Jonathan gently lift his daughter from the bed and carry her small body, wrapped in her blanket, in his arms. He crossed the street and slowly handed her lifeless form to the outstretched hands of the undertaker, who placed the precious bundle in the mortuary van. Jonathan stepped forward and laid her favourite doll, Raggedy Ann, next to her, to keep her company.

We stood in the street, watching the black van slowly drive down Ellsworth Avenue until it turned a corner, out of sight. No one moved. I felt a hollowed-out space in my chest. Here was the moment we'd been expecting for some time. Yet we had hoped, beyond reason, that it would never come.

Death and burial are times filled with required rituals. Some delay the anguish, while others kindle the agony. Jonathan and I went to Benjamin's Park Memorial Chapel to deal with the funeral arrangements. We were met by a tall man in a dark suit. He shook our hands and expressed his condolences in a quiet, mournful manner. He led us to a room furnished like a home living room except for the box of tissues on the coffee table. After offering tea or coffee, the funeral director explained the process. I knew it all too well. I had heard it all before, after the death of Scott, Marcia's Dad. There were the details to be decided, among them the death notices and their placement in newspapers and on the memorial chapel's website. There were the shiva arrangements and the choice of coffin.

"Would you like to use our chapel or have a graveside ceremony?" the director asked.

Jonathan opted for a graveside ceremony.

We rose from our easy chairs and were led into a room with a selection of coffins. Some were plain pine boxes. A few were so ornately decorated, they reminded me of grand pianos.

Jonathan chose a small pine coffin, one of the tiniest on display.

After all the details were reviewed, I asked for the bill. The undertaker handed it to me, and I glanced at the bottom line. "It looks like everything isn't on it," I said.

Softly, the director said, “Benjamin’s doesn’t charge for any services we provide for the death of an infant. There are only our actual disbursements.”

I thanked him in a cracked voice for this unexpected act of kindness.

Amazingly, about four hours after Sasha passed away, Pam went into heavy labour. Eleven hours later, early the next morning, she gave birth to Mia Ruby. She was born a month premature at Mount Sinai Hospital in downtown Toronto at 5:50 a.m. weighing 6 lb. 6 oz. I thought of the girls, Sasha and Mia, as two ships passing in the night.

Sasha’s funeral was a graveside service at Pardes Shalom, Temple Emanu-El section, on June 25, 2006. Mia, a week old, lay tucked in her stroller, next to the grave.

Jonathan, in a broken voice, asked the rabbi if he could be a pallbearer.

“It’s not a good idea,” the rabbi said. “In your grief you may stumble, and if you drop the coffin you’ll never forgive yourself.”

Marcia and I, with Pam’s brother, Kenny, and brother-in-law, Ofer, carried the small square coffin. It was barely large enough for the pallbearers to hold. Its tiny size highlighted the untimely loss of our beautiful two-year-old granddaughter.

Marcia gave the eulogy. In a heartbroken voice, she described what Sasha meant to us.

Your Mom and Dad call you their precious gift, Sasha the beautiful. This name refers not only to your gorgeous blonde curly hair and smiling eyes but your absolutely beautiful nature—you epitomize courage, feistiness, gentleness, vitality, and most importantly an incredible joy, which has touched all who have been privileged to know and therefore to love you. You inspire us and as a great teacher, you have imparted much wisdom in 24 months.

As she spoke, I knew I wouldn't have been able to give the eulogy without breaking down. I dabbed my eyes. Many others did the same.

"You are like a meteor," Marcia continued, "that shines very brightly and then moves through space in a swift trajectory; yet you will always shine in our hearts and minds."

I thought of Sasha's radiant smile whenever she greeted us or recognized something familiar to her.

"No words can adequately describe Pam and Jonathan's loving and selfless commitment to you. You have responded with joy in a circle of endless love." Marcia ended with, "*Hamba gahle,* go well, Sasha Bella. May you rest in peace. We love you so much and will always celebrate your life."

The prayers that followed became a blur. As each clod of earth thrown into the grave hit the coffin in our ancient tradition, the thump reverberated through me.

After more prayers we walked through the long line of mourners, shaking hands and giving hugs. We went to Pam and Jonathan's house for shiva.

It was surreal.

Downstairs friends and family congregated to offer their condolences and recite Kaddish, the prayer for the dead. Upstairs Pam was breastfeeding her new baby, experiencing the exhilaration of welcoming Mia while suffering the devastation of losing of her first-born, Sasha. With her were two nurses, Tessie and Riley, who had lovingly tended to Sasha.

We moved between two universes, mourning Sasha's absence and rejoicing at Mia's presence.

Each member of our family dealt with Sasha's passing in their own manner. There were so many ways to try to fill the aching need to remember.

Three-year-old Matthew, Sasha's cousin, wanted to know why

she had died. Alisa, his mother, asked a child psychologist what to say. She was advised not to say that Sasha had died because she was sick since Matthew and other children also get sick. So on the way to Sasha's last birthday party, Alisa had told Matthew that when Sasha was born, there were parts inside her body that were broken and the doctors were trying to fix them.

Matthew had asked, "You mean the blood and bones?"

"Yes, something like that, and that is why she has bandages on her arm and doesn't feel much like playing."

After Sasha died, Alisa explained that her body stopped working. "The doctors and Auntie Pam and Uncle Jonny tried hard but they couldn't fix what was broken. We won't be able to see Sasha again, and that's making us all very unhappy."

Matthew pursed his lips. "Can we give her an imaginary hug and blow her a kiss goodbye?"

His mother nodded.

With Mia's sudden arrival, Alisa had more explaining to do. She told him he'd been asleep when Mia was born.

Matthew had a hard time understanding that the two events were not related. People could be sad that Sasha was gone, yet happy that Mia was here. At first he couldn't grasp how you could feel more than one emotion at the same time, and it took a few days before he appeared to understand. Then he told his teachers and the kids at daycare about Sasha's passing and Mia's arrival.

Still, he hadn't stopped thinking about this. Again he asked, "Why did Sasha die?"

Alisa said she repeated exactly what she'd told him the first time.

"Can we still say her name?" he asked.

"Yes," Alisa said.

"Can we still think about her?"

"Of course."

"Can we imagine what she is doing?"

"Yes."

"That's good 'cause we can't really see what she's doing, but our hearts can, because hearts have things like telescopes to see far away."

Later that year came the unveiling of Sasha's tombstone.

Sean asked to ride with us and climbed into the back seat. "I hope I can handle being there, knowing that little Sashie is no longer here." Suddenly, as I was reversing out of the driveway, he called, "Stop. I can't go with you. Let me out."

"Surely you're coming to the unveiling?" I said.

"Yes, but I have to be on my own. I'll come on my own." He jumped out of the car.

At the cemetery, as we were walking to the graveside, I saw Sean arrive in his grey Ford Escort and stand quietly to the side.

I now understand more fully the pain that must have surged through him at the time. He had witnessed Sasha's fierce fight to survive, even as his own struggles tormented him. His grief for Sasha compounded his anguish.

The unveiling began with the song Sasha loved. "I Can Change the World with My Own Two Hands" was rendered by two talented musicians, guitarist David Wall, who had acted in *War Horse*, and vocalist Tressa Levaseur. The moving lyrics, written by Ben Harper, speak to the changes one person's resolve can achieve in making the world a better, kinder, brighter, safer place.

The white cotton sheet covering the pink granite headstone was slowly removed. The inscription read, "With my own two hands I can change the world." Sasha did change the world for us. Her courage and amazing joy showed us a way to relish life in the midst of pain. Engraved on the front of the headstone was her favourite doll, a small Raggedy Ann, with red yarn for hair and a triangular nose.

We were comforted by Rabbi Arthur Bielfeld, who had previously been there for us in our times of joy and sorrow, as he would be in the future, for Sean.

The thought of our beautiful Sasha lying in a cold grave next to deceased strangers was distressing. The cemetery only had limited space and each Temple member was allotted two sites. We approached the current rabbi of Temple Emanu-El, Deborah Landsberg, for special permission for adjoining sites for Marcia and me, Jonathan and Pam, so we could lie next to Sasha when our time came to join her.

The rabbi's response was spontaneous. "It's the least I can do," she said.

Moments like that are never forgotten.

As it was for Matthew, the question of remembering Sasha was vital to all the family. Jonathan created a website with videos and blog posts that reflected her inspiring journey. Jonathan and Pam set up the Sasha Bella Fund, through the SickKids Foundation, to support the parents of dying babies and children, and the Sasha Bella Award, an annual scholarship that recognized exemplary nursing practice and excellence in family-centred care.

Palliative care became an important issue for Jonathan and Pam. "The staff were very sensitive, but the time came when the doctors said they couldn't help us," Jonathan said. "To be an authentic place of healing, a hospital has to acknowledge and understand death. The two are not separate."

A few years later, Marcia and I, Sean and his friend Danusia walked along the windy shore at Robben Island, listening to the roar of the waves breaking on the rocks. On this remote island across from Cape Town, we visited the prison and small cell where Nelson Mandela had been jailed, as well as the limestone quarry where he had laboured in the blinding sun.

Before we left for South Africa, Pam had said, "Sasha Bella couldn't travel anywhere. Please bring back a few pebbles for her from your trip."

We spoke of our beloved Sashie. Marcia and I chose a few smooth stones. Sean also picked up pebbles, rubbed them between his thumb and forefinger, examined them carefully, discarded a few and kept the special ones. By placing them on her grave in Toronto, we would connect her spirit with the land of our birth, with Mandela and the freedom that finally came not only to South Africa, but to her as well, when she was released from pain.

I looked up into the blue sky flecked with wispy clouds and wondered if Sasha could read our thoughts.

"Sasha, where are you?" I called softly.

A silent lament for our beloved Sasha kept arising at unexpected times and places.

I remembered the cry of Emma Goldman, fierce fighter for political freedom, after her soulmate, Alex (Sasha) Berkmann, had taken his own life. I was struck by the coincidence that Emma Goldman's family had lived for a while near Kurland, the region of Latvia where my father, Julius, was born, and that she'd died at 295 Vaughan Road in Toronto, a five-minute walk from Jonathan and Pam's home.

Playwright Tony Kushner said of Emma Goldman, "She really lived her life on fire. And there's something utterly thrilling about that."

These words reminded me of the fiery spirit of our beloved granddaughter.

THIRTEEN

Providentia

Sean handed me a photo album opened to a picture of three small boys digging in the sand. "That one looks like me," he said. "What was I doing there?"

"You were building sand castles at Providentia, in Port Elizabeth, before any houses had been built there."

"Really? I looked pretty small then." He was small indeed, only three years old when the picture was taken.

"I took you to see the bulldozers moving earth to build roads and lay pipes for water and sewerage," I said. "You loved it when the driver picked you up and put you in his seat. You hummed like an engine, pulling at the steering levers, pretending you were scooping up the earth."

"One day," he said, "I would like to visit South Africa."

I nodded but doubted that would happen, even though Marcia and I would have loved to take Sean there. Whenever he saw an article in our daily Toronto newspaper about his birth country, he quickly brought it to my attention. However, from his late teen years, travelling with Sean was challenging at best. On a trip to the United States, many mornings he couldn't get up. At the last moment, he'd refuse to go on arranged outings, despite our urgent coaxing.

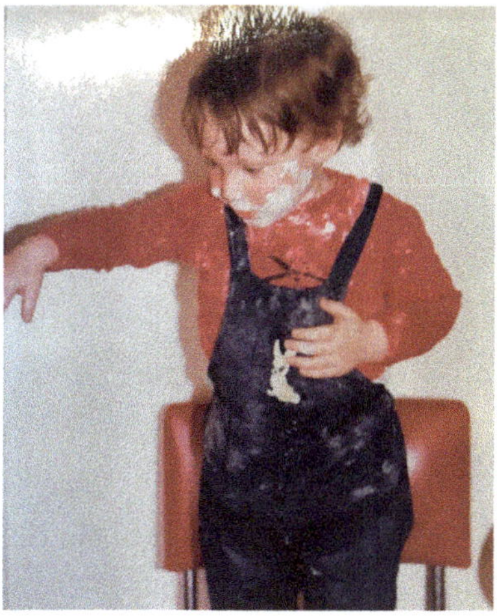

We'd even coined the term Spaghetti Factory Behaviour after the name of the restaurant in Toronto where he'd thrown such a tantrum that he had to be taken outside to quieten down. At the time, I thought he was being contrary. I'd since learned that there was much more to his outbursts than "bad behaviour."

He pointed to another picture of his boyhood self, his face and clothes covered in icing sugar. "Where was this taken?"

"In the kitchen at 37 Short Road, Port Elizabeth. That was your idea of fun."

He handed me a third photograph. I held it between my fingers and looked closely at Sean perched in a tree, staring anxiously at the camera.

Looking at the photo now, I recall Sean's painting I discovered after his death—the green baboon constrained by branches. I can't help but wonder if this image of him was the inspiration for his drawing fifteen years later.

In his late twenties Sean introduced us to Danusia. Tall and elegant, she embraced us with a spontaneous hug. "I'm so happy to meet you," she said. "Sean has told me much about you both." Danusia was delightful. She had a degree in theatre and an intense devotion to practicing yoga.

"It's wonderful they found each other," I told Marcia.

She nodded, smiling.

The relationship between Sean and Danusia blossomed. It seemed to me a new beginning, and Sean was the happiest we had seen him for many years.

Marcia and I were planning a trip to South Africa in December, when it would be summer there. "Why don't we ask them to join us?" I suggested. "Sean has always wanted to go, and if she comes, travelling might be easier for him." This also seemed to me a time to build on their happiness and encourage their relationship by providing the experience of travel and connection with our family's roots.

Marcia agreed, mentioning Sean's keen interest in the people from South Africa whom we had hosted. "He loved hearing their stories. They seemed to energize him."

Sean had told me one evening how much he admired people who strove to make a difference towards a better world, despite seemingly impossible challenges. I hoped that his reconnecting with them in South Africa would somehow inspire and invigorate him to overcome his own fears.

Danusia was receptive. "I'd love to come," she said, "as long as you understand that it doesn't mean a commitment on my part."

We understood. At the same time, we hoped that their travelling together would do exactly that—help cement their relationship. It would mean sharing joyful memories and sadder moments, exploring with them our hometown of Port Elizabeth and seeing family and special friends. And of course, a visit to South Africa wouldn't be complete without time spent at a game park.

Still, the next day, I questioned the wisdom of inviting them to join us. Sean's old meltdowns loomed in my mind. Would he get up at a reasonable time to accommodate a busy schedule? Would he adapt to a sudden change of plans? And then there was the pressure of four people travelling together. He had never been with Danusia for such a lengthy time. The risk was real; rather than furthering their relationship, the experience could tear it apart. And yet, we had asked, and they had accepted.

In the first week of our travels, driving along the streets of our old hometown of Port Elizabeth, I took on the role of chauffeur and tour guide. At every turn, faded images of our former lives suddenly resurfaced. I called out the names of the roads and pointed out buildings and landmarks such as St. George's Park.

"I played there on the swings and the jungle gym," Sean said.

I called their attention to a large white building, the maternity home at the Provincial Hospital. "Sean, that's where you were born. You were really small. I could hold you in one hand. Look at you now." We all smiled. I remembered my excitement as a nurse handed me the tiny wrapped bundle to hold.

My reminiscences careened in another direction as we passed an intersection on Cape Road. I caught myself about to say, "There's the spot where Robert Carruthers was hit by a car and killed." He was just thirteen, a school friend, riding home on his bicycle after sports. The last thing I wanted was for Sean to start dwelling on this tragedy.

As I recalled that childhood memory an icy chill stole over my body. Robert was my first friend who had ever died. In the barely one second that it takes to push down a bicycle pedal, he was gone, forever.

I went to see his parents. They both hugged me at the door. His mother's eyelids were red-rimmed. His father, also called Robert, said, "I want to show you our train collection." He led me to a room crisscrossed with miniature tracks and model locomotives, railway stations, farm houses, bridges and plastic animals. He let me run a locomotive on the railway tracks, adjusting the signals to avoid collisions.

When it was time for me to leave, they both said, "Please come and visit again."

"Of course," I answered, certain that I would. A few weeks later I phoned. There was no answer, and no answering machine. For some unremembered reason, I did not call again.

I had to forgive myself; not all of life's good intentions are fulfilled.

Many years later, after my own bereavement, when Sean's friends came to condole with us about the Sean they knew, I appreciated more fully how meaningful my visit must have been to Robert's grieving parents.

My mind flitted from thought to thought, feeling to feeling, as I tried to focus on driving along Cape Road. My emotions at the time of Robert's death kept surfacing, reminding me of Little Harry, my mother's baby brother, spilled from a car at the age of two and killed instantly. Like Robert's death, Little Harry's death was brutally unfair.

I pulled myself back to happier times, reminiscing aloud about our Saturday afternoon visits to the museum in Humewood. Our sons had been transfixed by the whale skeleton on the ceiling. After that, we'd drop by the aquarium to see the dolphins cavorting in the pool, topping off the day with crumpets, jam and cream in the cafeteria.

"Some of the places look familiar." Sean frowned. "I don't remember most of them. But I do remember the crumpets." He smiled broadly.

As I navigated the streets in our old hometown, I became acutely aware that returning to familiar places rekindles unexpected memories—some happy, some sombre that could not be shared.

The next day's drive along once-familiar roads awakened yet more memories. Sean wanted to visit 37 Short Road, where he had spent his baby years. We were warmly welcomed by Johan and Marieke, who had bought the house from us. They delighted in showing us around. As I walked from room to room, a feeling of other-worldliness crept over me. The reality of the present interleaved with memories of the past. The owners laughed as they pointed to Mark's name scratched under the desk in his old bedroom. Sean crawled under the desk to look and came out smiling. "It's amazing you found it," he said.

Johan and Marieke led us to a wine cellar and storeroom, where I had affixed a plaque to the door that detailed the history of the house.

"This house must've meant a lot to you," Sean said as he read it.

"I wanted later owners to know what had gone into the building," I said.

Wending our way through the house, I pointed out the oak components—the sliding doors, banisters and fielded panels that had been saved when the Market Square office building of Sir Lewis Richardson was torn down. Sean appeared unimpressed by this piece of history.

Marcia said softly, "It was a great pity that this beautiful building had to be demolished. At least we were able to save some of it for the future."

We slipped into Sean's old room. "This is where you slept in your crib and where I used to change your dirty diapers," I said. Sean and Danusia laughed. "One morning I found the head of Marcia's plastic hair-roller pin protruding from your bottom. Of course, I pulled it out. Marcia and I were horrified at the damage it could have caused and immediately took you to our family doctor. Dennis examined you and said you looked fine. I asked him how the hairpin could have wound its way through your gut. He just said, 'Don't ask.'"

Sean looked shocked. "Are you serious?"

I nodded. Unexpected details were helping to reconnect him with his childhood.

Outside I showed him the names of Jonathan, Mark and Kevin

scratched into the cement driveway.

What Sean noticed was an absence. "My name's not there."

"Sean, you weren't born yet."

He looked again at the driveway and laughed. "There's always a good reason why the youngest child is forgotten."

What could I say to that?

Sean asked to visit the graves of my parents in the North End Cemetery, and I was glad to see his interest; sadly, not many grandchildren ask to see the burial places of their grandparents.

At the whitewashed walls of the cemetery, Sean called out, "Wow. Look at this plaque. It says the stone was laid by Sir Lewis Richardson on January 16, 1924. Was he the same person whose building provided the oak panelling and doors in our house at 37 Short Road?"

I nodded. Sean now appeared to appreciate the distinctive features of our former home.

I opened the heavy metal gate and walked past Tahara House, where bodies were washed in a ritual act of purification before burial. I remembered standing in the small room next to the coffins, first Dad's and later Mom's, and being asked if I wanted to see the body for the last time. When I said yes, the coffin lid was slowly lifted and I found myself looking down at a pale face and shrouded body. The final goodbye.

To the right of the cemetery, an adjoining grey building with barred windows—the Port Elizabeth prison—loomed over us. The juxtaposition of the two sites had always struck me as incongruous: the one, interment for eternity; the other, incarceration during life.

We walked along a pathway that wound around the older, ornate tombstones until we got to the simple slabs denoting the graves of infants. Sean and I stopped to read their faded, moss-flecked inscriptions. I thought of the children's families, their pain as they'd lowered the small wooden caskets into the freshly dug graves, the unfulfilled lives that lay buried. I thought of Sasha's small coffin and Jonathan and Pam's wrenching grief.

Sean stood there gazing down. "I remember Sashie's funeral." He slowly moved away along the path.

At my parents' granite tombstones each of us placed a small pebble as a mark of remembrance. I had brought them from Toronto, to connect their resting places with our Canadian home. I recited, softly, the mourner's Kaddish, the prayer for the dead. The ritual required ten adult Jews to be present to say the prayer, but I knew that my parents would appreciate my intentions even if I couldn't comply with the proper ritual. I didn't need a prayer book as I had repeated this prayer many times for them, always in remembrance of their unstinting support. Their unbounded confidence in me had fuelled my inner strength to follow and realize many of my dreams. They had introduced me to a meaningful life and unfailingly pointed out significant guideposts. I would like to believe that I had done the same for all my sons.

I walked away slowly, oblivious to the other tombstones—thankful that I'd revisited their graves and that Marcia, Sean and Danusia were with me. As we drove off, Sean said quietly, "If it wasn't for them, I wouldn't be here."

Sean was keen to see the sign "Blumbergweg," meaning

"Blumberg Road," in Providentia. "Take a photo of me standing there," he said. So I did.

"How come our name is on the sign?"

I was the developer of Providentia and Lovemore Heights, I explained, but was embarrassed to name a street after me. Our family name was chosen by the developer and the land surveyor of the suburb next door, Pari Park. "I did name Marcia Way after your mother for being so supportive of me through all the ups and downs of the real estate market in Port Elizabeth."

We both laughed.

Sean listened, enthralled, as I described the land that became Providentia back in the 1970s, when it was still a bushy area with a few grazing cows, sheep and horses.

The road sign was significant in more ways than one. It acknowledged my family and also my involvement in developing the region. I was pleased that Sean took pleasure in posing for the photo.

We drove along the wide roads of the nearby suburb of Lovemore Heights, formerly a windswept barren hill on the outskirts of the city. Between the elegant homes, panoramic views opened up of the green foliage, streets and shimmering buildings in the city below.

Sean asked, "Can anyone own a house and live here?" I explained that since the democratic election in 1994 and the abolition of the Group Areas Act, racial separation was no longer required by law. Sadly, that wasn't so when these suburbs were developed.

Sean asked, "Where are we going next?"

"To see something very different," I said. "How the apartheid system destroyed a community."

When we arrived at South End I visualized through dream-like memories the hustle and bustle of what was once a vibrant, multicultural community. I had gone there many times with my parents to shop for food. The small, family-run stores had all disappeared when the suburb was bulldozed under apartheid's Group Areas Act. The government forcibly relocated the "non-White" inhabitants, scattering them to distant areas bordering the city.

"Look how parts of South End have now been rebuilt into a bland housing estate," I said. How ironic: while I was building suburbs in Port Elizabeth, the government was bulldozing whole communities in the same city.

At the foot of Walmer Road, I pointed out the site of Imperial Fruiterers where my parents used to buy our fresh produce. "My big treat was that my mother let me fill a packet of multicoloured sweets from rows on the shelves. She wasn't too happy about my choices and used to say, 'The sugar will eat away your teeth.'"

"Now I know why you've had so many dental implants," Sean quipped.

I waved excitedly down Walmer Road. "That's where my mother chose fish for dinner. She could tell from the eyes of the dead fish if it was from the morning's haul or the previous day's. She brought the whole fish home, descaled and filleted it. She loved to eat boiled fish head."

"Ugh." Sean pulled a face.

"See that vacant lot on the left?" I slowed down as we passed. "A man called Nathan had a tailor shop there. When I was a kid it was a mystery to me what work he really did. The same two suits hung on the wall for months on end." I could still picture the thread-bare carpets in Nathan's two rooms, the first with its worn linoleum shop's counter and dusty shelves. In the back room, an employee wearing a red fez appeared busy, stitching a jacket or a pair of trousers. "I asked my father if the store was a front for something, like selling marijuana. He told me that Nathan ran a *fafi* operation."

"What's that?" Sean asked.

"It's an illegal numbers game that deals with figures from one to thirty-six. Each one has a name or character. They have draws, maybe twice a day, and people can win money."

"Didn't the police try to catch him?" Sean asked.

"Yes, they tried, but they couldn't build a case because he kept no paper records. He was a genius. Everything was in his head."

Nathan reminded me once again of the diverse characters who worked and lived in what had once been a remarkable, bustling suburb.

"Wow," Sean said the next morning at breakfast, "You're packing a lot into this trip." He was right, but Marcia and I wanted to make the trip as meaningful as possible for them. We were trying to strike a balance between seeing landmarks and visiting people. I considered relationships to be the most memorable.

Sean's remark alerted me that our busy schedule could be too taxing for him. Thereafter I watched for tell-tale signs, from yawning and bleary eyes to an unshaven face, ruffled hair, rumpled clothes or loss of appetite, that could indicate he was succumbing to stress.

Thus far, all was well. Yet we rose each morning knowing there was no certainty how the day would unfold.

Sean asked to meet the family of our former housekeeper, Eunice Mafanga: Veronica, Wendy and their children. Eunice had passed away a few years after we'd emigrated. The day we received a telegram saying she had died, we were shocked and upset. We reminisced about the vital role she had played in our family for many years. All we could do from Canada was to assist financially with the burial arrangements, honouring her according to her customs and traditions.

Marcia and I had met Eunice's son, Gladman, and his wife, Wendy, on a prior visit, and learnt the sobering details about Gladman's struggles. "There are few jobs here. I only get work from time to time." They had two children and had adopted another from their extended family.

Two years after we'd met Gladman, we were awoken at 2 a.m. by the shrill ring of our phone. In between sobs, Wendy told me that Gladman had died. He had suffered an acute asthma attack and was rushed to hospital. Tragically, he wasn't provided with the oxygen he needed in time. That left Wendy as the sole breadwinner for their three children. As I expressed my condolences, I felt the presence of Eunice asking me to help provide for them; so Marcia and I did.

Before we left Toronto, Sean suggested that we take a computer with us for Wendy. "I'm sure they'll appreciate it."

One of Sean's happiest moments in South Africa was his time at Wendy's home in New Brighton, when she invited us for tea. He and Danusia installed the computer while the family watched, enthralled.

Later, we took Wendy to Korsten to buy school uniforms and supplies for her children. I parked outside the store and waited in the rented car so it wouldn't be left unattended. A man in tattered trousers held up by a knotted cord swayed up to my door, waving his fingers and mumbling. I opened the window a crack and smelled the blast of alcohol. He told me it was "dangerous" to be there and offered to protect me. I rummaged in my pocket and handed him a few coins. He smiled with a gap-toothed grin, revealing his remaining yellowed teeth. After thanking me with exaggerated gestures, my guardian sat down on the curb. He soon keeled over, fast asleep.

We gathered for dinner at a steakhouse called Catalina Spur. I sensed Eunice looking down on us, smiling. She would be proud of her family. Much had changed since we'd last seen her. Now in a post-apartheid era, we could all sit together in a restaurant that had once been reserved strictly for Whites and was now free from racial barriers.

Later that night our hosts, Merle and Arnie, were aghast when I told them we had gone to Korsten. "It's very dangerous," Arnie said. "I wouldn't go there. You're lucky you weren't robbed. Of course, you wouldn't know, you've been away a long time."

I didn't mention my protector.

Sean spoke up. "At least where we're going tomorrow we won't be robbed, although we might be eaten alive."

FOURTEEN

Freedom behind Fences

The gates of Shamwari Game Reserve swung open and a guard dressed in khaki waved us through. We entered a deceptively peaceful world far removed from high-rises, traffic lights, congested roads, and city dwellers, hurrying and scurrying, stressed by the daily grind of survival. Yet underneath the tranquility of Shamwari lurked an animal ferocity.

We arrived at our lodge, Eagles Crag, early and needed to wait until it was vacated by departing guests. Marcia reminded us that Lisa, Mark's wife, was scheduled to undergo surgery that day. In response, Danusia asked us to sit in a circle and hold hands while she guided us through a meditation. We prayed that the soul of Shamwari would embrace our family in our distant home and protect Lisa. We later called Mark and were relieved to hear that all had gone well.

That afternoon from our deck at the lodge, we spotted eagles soaring against the backdrop of a craggy rock face. One gracefully glided before us then slowly disappeared behind the ridge.

Early the next morning with the world on the cusp of dawn, the four of us joined our guide, Jacob, for our nature drive. Sean walked up to him. "We would love to see the big five. Do you think that's possible?"

"Yes, that's my goal—to show you elephants, Cape buffalo, rhinos, lions, and hopefully a leopard." He joked that today all shooting is done through a camera lens or smartphone. In a more serious tone, he warned us that the animals were dangerous. "When we stop to look at them, always stay in the vehicle. We don't want any of you to become a morning snack or get trampled into mush." He pointed to his gun on the floor. "Just in case," he said.

We clambered onto the open tarpaulin-topped game vehicle, Sean and Danusia in the front seats. Bundled in blankets, we bounced along rugged roadways gouged out of the veld. Wisps of mist were floating in the distance. As the sun rose over the faraway *koppies* and the air warmed, I let my blanket drop to the seat.

A herd of warthogs suddenly scampered across the open grasslands. They were the unattractive members of the pig family, with protruding tusks, large heads and almost hairless, dull grey skin. The thick growths on the males' faces resembled warts. The hogs scurried through the grass in a line, tails erect, the tips waving like small pennants.

Near a pool we encountered the first of the big five—a herd of elephants with white, curved tusks and fan-shaped ears, splashing and cavorting in the water, waving their long trunks. Their wet, dark hides glistened in the sun. Sean clicked away, training his lens on an elephant calf at the water's edge. He turned and said, "Isn't he cute?"

A bull lumbered towards us, drawing closer and closer. The majestic animal towered above our vehicle. All at once, our guide, sensing we'd reached the limits of our welcome, slammed the vehicle into gear and accelerated away.

We then passed by grazing springboks. Their coats varied from a pale to rich cinnamon brown, with patches of white. A few leaped away gracefully as our vehicle approached. Others continued grazing, seemingly unperturbed. Occasionally, they gazed our way, warily flicking their pointed ears.

When we stopped for refreshments on a hill overlooking the panoramic landscape, Sean and Danusia stood apart, but I could see them smiling broadly. Moments like that amply justified our decision to invite them to accompany us. Sean was the happiest I'd seen him in years.

Back in the vehicle, the game drive continued. We scrutinized the landscape for sightings. Jacob pointed to a small herd of buffalo, grazing. "Number two of the big five," he called out.

The crackling radio alerted Jacob to the whereabouts of something special. He drove at breakneck speed to where the animal had last been sighted.

"There it is." Jacob pointed.

The black rhino was partially hidden behind bushes. He raised his head and stared at us. He looked prehistoric, like a creature that had trod the earth for millions of years, roaming without fear. Jacob told us of the peril the rhinos were facing. Despite efforts by guards to protect them, armed poachers with tracking devices tranquilized them and hacked off their horns, leaving them bleeding, to wake up and die an agonizing death. The horns were trafficked and sold at astronomic prices for medicinal purposes and carvings.

Sean turned to Danusia. "That's terrible." She nodded.

As we sped off, Jacob said under his breath, "I hope he doesn't charge us."

Sean pointed and called out, "What's that beautiful bird?" Jacob said it was a *bokmakierie.* I leaned forward and strained to detect the bird partly hidden among leafy branches, its olive-green body and yellow-tipped black tail the perfect camouflage. I was surprised that Sean had seen it and pleased that he was so deeply engrossed in the experience that little escaped his attention.

We shuddered to a halt. "Look," Jacob said. "A lion feeding on an antelope. You can tell it's a male by the mane around his face."

Sean and Danusia took photos, one after another. This had to be an unforgettable moment for them.

We felt safe, yet all around our open vehicle dangers lurked. No wonder the loaded gun was within easy reach.

Again and again we raced up and down hills and over rutted paths, hoping for further encounters with the animals. Midday was fast approaching, and Jacob turned back to the lodge. "At least you've seen four out of five," he said. I felt a surge of disappointment. Sean and Danusia had not seen a leopard.

Jacob pointed to a martial eagle soaring gracefully, high in the blue sky. We passed giraffes, elegantly munching leaves from the tree tops.

Suddenly, we jolted to a stop. "Look," Jacob called.

We stared.

"There, in the grass patch. A leopard. See the black rosette spots on her fur?" Jacob pointed out the long tail curving upward, ending in a unique white tip so that cubs could identify their mother.

We returned to the lodge, happy to have seen the big five.

As we were having dinner Sean said, "I loved the cute warthogs, birds, and buck all wandering unhindered." He paused. "Of course, I try to forget that while they seem free, they're all enclosed by electric fences."

That evening, I gazed transfixed at the golden veld under the great orange sky. I thought of the golden yellow flowers of the smudging herb *imphepho*, used by traditional healers, *sangomas*, for medicinal purposes. The smoke is inhaled as a ritual incense to induce a trance state for communicating with the ancestors. There was no need for me to inhale that smoke to transport me to another world—I was already mesmerized. For a few moments, I became part of the landscape, captivated by the deep soul of Africa.

In my reverie, my hopes for Sean also grew keen. I hoped his and Danusia's relationship would outlast their gasps of wonder as they revelled in the breathtaking scenery and the magic of viewing majestic animals from the safety of a game vehicle.

At breakfast the next day on our first morning in Cape Town, I was reluctant to be the bearer of disappointing news: some Robben Island trips had been cancelled due to stormy seas. Sean had mentioned before we left Toronto that what he wanted to see most was the place where Nelson Mandela had been imprisoned.

As we drove to the Victoria and Albert Waterfront, Sean kept saying, "I hope the trip is still on."

At the Nelson Mandela Gateway to Robben Island we found a long lineup for the ferry. And our booked trip had been cancelled. I saw Sean's crestfallen look. "We'll try our best to get on," I said. He barely acknowledged my comment.

Marcia and I walked to the front of the line to the ticket collector near the gangplank. We explained that we had travelled from Canada and that it would be a terrible disappointment for our son and friend to miss this experience. She looked at us skeptically. I added, "Nelson Mandela is our son's hero and this visit is the highlight of the whole trip."

She smiled. "Okay, I'll see what I can do. Not everyone arrives.

Stand there." She pointed to a spot a few feet away.

We watched the long line slowly embarking. "Looks like we won't get on," Sean said.

When the last person had boarded, the ticket collector turned to us. "You can get on."

We settled in our seats, facing a monitor that screened the history of Robben Island. It was Christmas, and there was a festive mood among the passengers. I could hear only snatches of the commentary above the animated voices of adults, screaming children, and the din of the engines as the ferry cut through the choppy Atlantic Ocean.

At the island we landed at Murray's Harbour and were directed to a bus. I pointed to an arch with the word "Robbeneiland" and the slogan in Afrikaans and English, "*Ons dien met trots,* We serve with pride." On the left side were the words "*Welkom*" and "Welcome."I thought of the reaction of the prisoners as they faced the irony of those phrases. Sean said it reminded him of the infamous concentration camp signs. Of course the difference was significant. The concentration camps were death camps, while here on this confining island, the human spirit was attacked, leaving the bodies alive.

Aboard the bus, the festive air of the visitors slowly evaporated as the guide detailed the harshness of apartheid and the brutal treatment of political prisoners. Sean, seated in front of us with Danusia, had his camera at the ready; he didn't want to miss anything.

The bus stopped for a few minutes at a cemetery where about 1,500 lepers were buried. They had been ripped away from their families to spend the rest of their days in this inhospitable place.

Seventeen years after our visit, having lived through Covid 19, I better understand the necessity of isolating the sick to protect the rest of the community. In both instances, the disease was spread through contact with nasal and mouth droplets, although leprosy was not as contagious. Unlike leprosy at the time, the Covid 19 virus could end in recovery and a return to society or in a relatively quick death. Lepers were ostracized for life, which must have added to their heart-wrenching pain.

The lime quarry was our next stop. On the small hill to the left we saw a cave and near the bus a heap of stones. Our guide explained the great significance of the site in the struggle for political rights in South Africa.

Nelson Mandela and the other political prisoners worked in the open quarry in the relentless sun. Their eyes, especially Mandela's, were badly affected by the sun's glare and its reflection off the white limestone. The back-breaking work was designed more to destroy their spirit than provide any functional benefit.

I recalled seeing the play, *The Island,* which was devised collaboratively in 1973 by Athol Fugard, John Kani, and Winston Ntshona. The two actors, John and Winston, mimed the digging of sand to fill a wheelbarrow, which they pushed from one side of the island to the other, emptied, and refilled. Perspiration poured down their faces as they reenacted the futile, demoralizing task. In like manner, in the Greek myth, Sisyphus was doomed to push an immense boulder to the top of a hill, only for it to roll down again.

Our guide pointed to the cave and explained that the prisoners ate in there. It was also used as a toilet. Inside were two buckets where they could relieve themselves. The White guards would not enter the cave. "Maybe the stink was too much for them," our guide said with a smile. "Or maybe, as they were brought up during apartheid, they thought they were forbidden to enter Black toilets in the same way Blacks couldn't enter White toilets." A few people laughed.

Some prisoners were illiterate. Nelson Mandela and others managed to smuggle in books and wrote with sticks on the ground. They adopted the slogan "each one, teach one." They took every opportunity to uplift and educate, engaging in vigorous discussion as they sat in circles in the quarry chopping limestone. The site became known as the Robben Island University.

The guide spoke of the reunion on the island in February 1995, a year after the legal end of apartheid. About 1,200 former political prisoners gathered. Mandela broke away from the crowd, picked up a stone and walked away slowly, placing it at the entrance to the quarry. The others followed, vowing to continue this ritual of remembrance every five years until the last political prisoner had died.

Through the window Sean directed his lens at the pile of rocks, the stones added one at a time, a memorial to those who toiled in the lime quarry and a symbol of the triumph of the human spirit.

As the bus drove away, I leaned forward and said to Sean and Danusia, "Maybe this was where democracy was born in South Africa." They both nodded.

At the grey-stone former maximum-security prison, another guide introduced himself as Spars. He spoke earnestly, never smiling, but laced his presentation with flashes of humour.

"In 1981, when I was sixteen years old, I joined the military wing of the African National Congress, *uMkhonto we Sizwe*, the Spear of the Nation. I was charged the following year with terrorism." He paused. "But don't be afraid—I won't terrorize you." Sean laughed with the others.

In a deadpan voice he said, "You are free to take photos. You are free to ask questions. You are allowed to smile." We all laughed.

Spars spent five years imprisoned on Robben Island. "They stripped away our names and gave us a number. Nelson Mandela's was 46664." The guards doled out thin trousers and short-sleeved shirts. In the biting cold, some political prisoners contracted diseases like TB and pneumonia and died soon after they were released.

The few letters they were allowed were heavily censored with most of the content deleted or scissored out. Few visitors were allowed. To crush their morale even further, some prisoners were told they were to be released. At the last moment, the guards claimed they had made a mistake.

Spars pointed to a small garden in the corner of the courtyard. There Nelson Mandela had buried the draft of his book *Long Walk to Freedom* in plastic cocoa containers. The guards found it, but fortunately he had given a copy to a fellow prisoner, Mac Maharaj. Released in 1976, Maharaj smuggled the manuscript to the outside world. After Mandela's release from prison, nearly twenty years later, the book was published, having travelled its own long journey. After the democratic elections of 1994, Mandela appointed Maharaj minister of transport. "That was no surprise," Spars said. "He had proven himself good at transporting information!"

As we walked to the cells, I pointed out to Sean and Danusia a large photo of a former political prisoner, Billy Nair. On an adjoining plaque we read: "In 1964, we froze. Ask anyone, we froze as if we were in an ice box from morning to evening. We froze, froze, froze, all the time. Even at night when we were sleeping." I turned to Sean. "He was here with Nelson Mandela. His brother, Jay Nair, lives in Toronto. Every time I see Jay he proudly mentions his brother's fight against apartheid and the recognition he later received." Sean smiled.

At the cell Nelson Mandela had occupied, we stopped and stared at the barred window, the thin mat on the floor, the blankets rolled up neatly in a small pile against the wall, the small stool, the aluminum-coloured mug on a plate, and the brown metal bucket with a lid. In the *Long Walk to Freedom*, Mandela recalled: "I could walk the length of my cell in three paces. When I lay down, I could feel the wall with my feet and my head grazed the concrete at the other side."

Sean and I waited until the crowd moved on. I wanted to absorb the moment, to let it remain with me as a symbol of Mandela's courage in facing adversity and the impact of his spirit of reconciliation on South Africa and the rest of the world. Sean's reflections may have been similar.

As we passed an empty cell with its door ajar, Sean entered and sat on the small wooden stool. He slowly lifted the lid off the brown bucket and looked at the smaller bucket inside. He then replaced the lid and walked out.

Spars thanked us for coming. "As a political prisoner, I have reconciled with my captors," he said. "I don't hold a grudge against the people who victimized, interrogated and assassinated our leadership. We fought for peace for all those years and cannot now turn this country into a war zone. We want South Africans to be returned to the international community that helped them during the dark years of oppression."

As we walked slowly to the ferry Sean said, "I think you and Mom met Nelson Mandela. Is that right?" I told him that Marcia and I first saw him at a reception in September 1998 at Toronto's Royal York Hotel. Four years later, in November 2002, we met Nelson Mandela and his wife, Graca Machel, at a private reception. Mandela was eighty-three. He seemed physically frail but very alert. We had a few minutes to speak with them and expressed our appreciation for what he had achieved for South Africa and the example of reconciliation that he set for the rest of the world. He smiled and acknowledged what I said, even though he must have heard similar sentiments expressed many times.

Sean asked, "What impact do you think Nelson Mandela made?"

"He fought against oppression, survived twenty-seven years of harsh imprisonment and convinced his captors that it was time for reconciliation," I said. "He prevented a blood-bath in South Africa. For me he's a courageous man and an inspiring hero."

Sean stood still. "Yes. To me he is also a moral hero."

I was looking forward to the coming week when we, and especially Sean, would reconnect with people he admired and who, despite all obstacles, had fought to improve the lives of the disadvantaged in South Africa. Hope against hope, Marcia and I prayed that Sean, too, would find inspiration to guide him and courage to uplift him.

FIFTEEN

Langa My Dive

I feared that one morning Sean would blurt out that he'd done enough—that all he wanted to do was lounge by the pool. We'd planned a busy week in Cape Town, reconnecting with family and friends. So far, all had gone well—I hoped it would continue and that the experience would invigorate Sean to enter into a new phase of his life.

We were staying at the Vineyard Hotel in Newlands to be near Marcia's aunt and uncle, Irma and Selwyn. Sean was excited to see them again. They were the only African family members to attend any of our four bar mitzvahs in Toronto. "They came to mine," Sean told Danusia.

He seemed proud of that fact.

Marcia had developed a special bond with them and kept in close contact from Toronto. After Sean's passing, Irma was one of the few people Marcia spoke to regularly in her grief.

Marcia, Irma, Sean and Danusia all shared a common interest in theatre and delighted in discussing memorable productions.

In the study Sean looked at photos of Selwyn dressed in his white cricket gear. He was intrigued to hear that Selwyn had once been an ardent cricketer. "I thought everyone in South Africa only played rugby!" he said smiling.

"He more than played cricket," I said. "Selwyn was president of the Western Province Cricket Union." Sean looked impressed, although I doubted he knew what it meant. An avid sports fan, he listened enthralled as Selwyn explained how to bowl a "googly."

Selwyn was a role model in my life. He had given me the courage to become a real estate developer in Port Elizabeth, back when I doubted my ability. "You can do it," he reassured me. Those four words became my mantra. But I was far from Selwyn's sole admirer. Throughout South Africa he was respected for his contribution to the housing industry and the creation of new towns. Selwyn had pioneered the concepts of life-cycle housing, group housing, specialized housing for the elderly, zero building lines and the planning of new towns within an overall architectural philosophy.

To Marcia, Selwyn was her beloved uncle. Irma and Selwyn, to all of us, were close and loving family.

Other much-loved family members included Louis and Joyce, Marcia's uncle and aunt, her cousins Daphne, Marion and Renaye, and Renaye's husband, David. On every visit to Cape Town, one of Marcia's cousins organized a dinner to bring us all together.

That evening at Renaye and David's home, Sean whispered in my ear, "Is he really *the* David Kramer?"

I nodded. "I'll tell you about him later tonight."

In years past, I had seen our gentle cousin transformed on stage into a human dynamo, his powerful rasping voice and guitar electrifying his wildly cheering audience. David was a South African icon, one of the country's most popular singers, songwriters and directors. Wherever he went he was instantly recognized, thanks to his characteristic red *veld skoene*, the traditional South African walking shoes and his pork-pie hat.

Back at the hotel, Marcia told Sean and Danusia about David's first musical production, *District Six,* co-produced with Renaye in collaboration with the legendary South African musician, Taliep Petersen. We saw the musical in 1988 at the Edinburgh International Festival. It captured the vibrancy of life in District Six, the once mixed-race suburb in Cape Town, and the heart-wrenching breakup of the community and the government's forced removal and relocation of its Coloured residents during apartheid.

We had pointed out to Sean and Danusia the barren land that was once District Six as we drove along De Waal Drive.

David wrote songs about people who'd been forgotten and marginalized during apartheid. He also championed guitarists with unique finger-picking styles in remote outposts like the semi-desert areas of the Karoo. Through the performing arts, David Kramer had shone a light on the vibrancy of mixed-race communities and the incredible unsung talent in this country.

"I'm sorry you didn't get to meet Louis and Joyce," I said. "Last time we were here, they drove from Worcester over the Du Toitskloof Pass to be with us. Louis was nearly a hundred years old."

"Wow," Sean said. "What keeps him going?"

"His incredible sense of humour, love of people, and optimism," I said.

I had asked Louis whether he'd been concerned about driving over the precipitous mountain pass.

He looked at me in mock surprise. "Why should I be worried? The other drivers should be scared."

With a mischievous grin, Louis added, "You know, my doctor died. My dentist died. My accountant died. My pharmacist died. I think God has forgotten about me."

"No, Dad." Daphne laughed. "He didn't forget. You're deaf, and you didn't hear when he called you."

I told Sean about Louis's magic ingredient. He had once owned a Coca Cola bottling plant and had been honoured among the beverage fraternity as "the oldest Coca Cola bottler in the country"—living proof of the slogan, "Things go better with Coke."

Sean looked directly at me. "I wish I could be optimistic. I was once, but I don't feel like that anymore."

His comment distressed me.

We reconnected with our friend, the playwright and theatre director Fatima Dike. Sean and Danusia had met Fatts, as she was affectionately called, at our home in Toronto and were excited to see her again.

With Fatts as our guide, we drove through her home township of Langa, twenty minutes from the centre of Cape Town. The narrow lanes were filled with shacks made of corrugated steel, boards, scraps of wood and shipping containers—makeshift homes that baked in the summer and froze in the winter. We were struck by the stark contrast between the rank poverty of the townships and the affluence of suburban Cape Town, with its magnificent homes and green lawns, luxurious high-rises and hotels, shopping centres, and exclusive neighbourhoods with houses perched dramatically on hillsides reserved, during apartheid, for Whites.

Yet in Langa, street life was pulsating. Food vendors hovered over drums filled with open fires, grey smoke swirling as they grilled bulls' brains, testicles, tongues, pig's trotters, goat's ears and the ever-popular sheep heads. Nothing was wasted. Brightly decorated *spazas,* neighbourhood stores, operated out of repurposed shipping containers or shacks often attached to houses. Among the multitude of unregulated small businesses and trades were food kiosks, beauty salons, backyard mechanics, panel beaters, shoe repair shops, and carpenters. Fatts explained that while more than sixty percent of the residents of Langa were unemployed in the conventional sense, they managed to eke out a living in the informal economy.

As we drove along Fatts said, "Don't be deceived by what you have seen. There is much more to Langa." She directed our attention to an area of sturdy upper-class homes, where fencing provided both protection and decoration. She pointed out her solid brick house, where many generations of her family had lived.

"Fatts," Sean asked, "Why don't you move to some other area like Newlands, Wynberg or Claremont?"

Langa, she said, was home. With the fall of apartheid and the removal of residential restrictions, some affluent residents chose to remain in Langa—it was their community, the place where they had grown up, raised their families, and, like her, had put down roots.

We parked on the main street near the Guga S'Thebe Cultural Centre. Its entrance, covered in bright ceramic ornamentation, stood in striking contrast to the buildings and street life elsewhere. Fatts walked us through the vibrant spaces for pottery, dance, children's theatre and a drumming circle. Beaming, she told us that the centre enriched the Langa community and provided a home in the Western Cape for arts, culture and heritage. In one studio, students were molding and sculpting coloured sand, creating animal and human scenes. People hugged her and warmly welcomed us, whom she introduced as her friends from Canada.

Sean asked what *Guga S'Thebe* meant. Fatts explained that the

Xhosa idiom *Guga S'thebeKudala Usophulela* praises an aging serving platter for its lasting and friendly service. Just as the platter served many generations and people from all walks of life, so too will the centre prepare and nourish future generations. "The centre provides a lifeline for the community," she said, "especially for those who live and breathe arts and culture."

The site of the building, Fatts added, was historically significant in the struggle against apartheid, as it is situated close to Maranga Square, where in 1954 thousands of people burned their passes before marching to the city.

Danusia asked, "What do you mean by passes?"

For a moment I was surprised at her question. Then I realized that all this was new to her and Sean, having both grown up in Toronto.

Fatts explained that in 1952 the government passed a law requiring all African men over the age of sixteen to carry a Reference Book, replacing the previous Passbook. It contained information about the person: a photograph, fingerprint, address, name of the employer and how long the person had been employed. Employers often entered an evaluation of the pass-holder's behaviour. This book, she said, was one of the most hated symbols of apartheid. If it was lost or stolen or absentmindedly left behind, the person could be thrown in jail or exiled to a rural area.

Inscribed on a street pillar outside the centre was a quotation from Fatts. Sean read it aloud: "Langa My Dive. I was born in this Township. I grew up in this street. There are 10 houses on this block. We played this potholed street into the ground. Fatima Dike." He said, "It reflects the love the people in Langa have for Fatts."

Fatts glanced at her watch. "It's lunch time. We're going to a very special restaurant."

Sean laughed. "Do they serve smileys?" I asked what he meant. He explained that "smileys" refer to the grotesque grinning of the sheep's head as it turns golden brown during cooking. Sean had done his research.

"If you're lucky," Fatts told him, "I'll teach you to love it like we do in the townships."

Sean pulled a wry smile.

At Lelapa Restaurant, we were welcomed by Mama Sheila, the owner, and her daughter, Monica.

"*Lelapa* means home," Fatts said with a smile.

The buffet table overflowed with braised kudu shanks, ostrich stroganoff, chicken fillets, *brinjal* (eggplant) and marrow, not to mention countless salads. Fortunately, or unfortunately, smileys were not on offer! We heaped our plates and ate, tapping our feet to the rhythms of the African band that enlivened the restaurant with marimba and drumming. On our way out, Mama Sheila gave each of us a hug. I again felt the remarkable outpouring of hospitality extended to perfect strangers, as friends of Fatts.

Fatts's phone rang. She answered in Xhosa. "That was my sister Nomahlubi," Fatts said when the call ended. "She invited us for dinner tonight."

"You mean the archbishop's wife?" Sean asked.

Fatts laughed. "Yes, she's married to Archbishop Winston Hugh Njongonkulu Ndungane," she said rhyming off his full name. "He's the one who succeeded Bishop Tutu, the winner of the Nobel Prize."

The large iron gates at 16-29 Bishopscourt Drive swung open onto a long driveway flanked by hydrangeas. At the end of drive sat the imposing house of the Archbishop of Cape Town.

Nomahlubi met us at the entrance and introduced us to her husband. The archbishop greeted us warmly and led us to the patio where he was busy grilling lamb, steak and *boerewors*, the traditional South African farmer's sausage. At first I found it incongruous that he was dressed casually, sporting short pants rather than imposing clerical vestments. Even an archbishop, I realized, has to relax. I sank into a recliner and sipped my cold Castle beer, enjoying the lush garden's multicoloured flowers and the appetizing aroma wafting from the barbeque.

Luswazi, Nomahlubi's son, approached Sean and me. He was in his twenties and had studied in America. Now he was trying to start a telecommunication company, but it was tough going. He hoped to attract investors by parlaying his connections.

On the way back to our hotel, Sean commented on the vast difference between life in the townships and the suburbs of Cape Town, particularly that of Bishopscourt.

When I next glanced in the rearview mirror, Sean had fallen asleep with his head nestled against Danusia's shoulder—taking a break after a long day.

Marcia and I invited Fatts to join us for breakfast the next morning. Sean and Danusia hadn't yet come down. We called their room and Danusia answered. "Sorry we're late. We'll be another ten minutes or so."

When they joined us, Sean mumbled an apology without smiling. He walked over to the large buffet and stared at the offerings, finally helping himself to a dry bagel. As he pecked at it, I resisted the parental urge to ask, "Is that all you're having?"

Marcia and I had talked about slowing down the pace and looked at what we could leave out of sightseeing. We had already taken them for the ride by cableway to the top of Table Mountain, followed by Boulder Beach. They were enchanted by the African penguins, waddling near us in their black-and-white plumage.

We had also visited the University of Cape Town, which meant so much to Marcia and me. From its campus, nestled on the slopes of Devil's Peak, we gazed in awe at the panoramic view of Cape Town below.

"I must show you the Student Representative Council's chamber," I said.

"They're tired," Marcia cautioned. "They've seen enough already. Is that really necessary?"

"It will just take a minute," I said.

Reluctantly, they followed me into the building and over to the framed black-and-white photos of former office bearers hanging on the dark-panelled walls of the council board room. I couldn't resist an unseemly surge of pride as I pointed to the one that included me.

Sean and Danusia eventually found my youthful face. With a touch of disappointment, I watched them gaze less than enthusiastically at the faded photo.

As Sean nibbled at his dry bagel, I realized that less sightseeing might have been better.

But Fatts announced that she had a special surprise planned for Sean.

He looked up guardedly. "What do you mean?"

Fatts laughed. "You'll see. I'm not giving away the secret until we get there."

In the car Fatts said, "Sean, do you remember that? Marcia went out one afternoon, and when she got back, Pat Matalongwe said, 'Marcia, you didn't lock your cupboards—you left them all unlocked!'" Sean perked up.

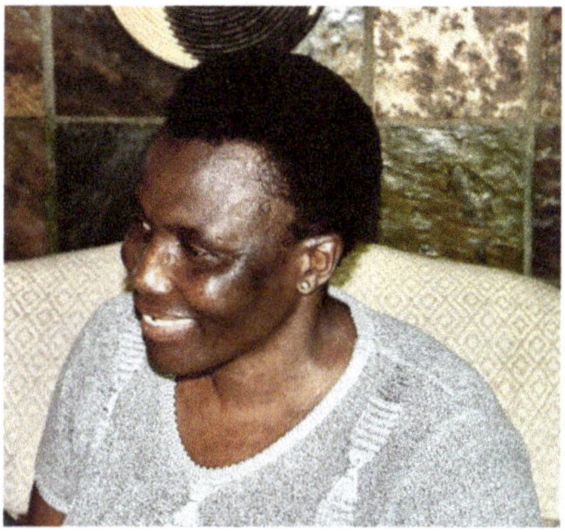

In apartheid South Africa, Pat had been a domestic worker and was used to her employer, the "white madam," locking her cupboards. In South Africa, as elsewhere, domestic workers were often grossly underpaid, worked long hours, and on occasion had to help themselves to flour, sugar, cereals, and other staples to bring home to feed their families.

"I never locked my food cupboards when we lived in South Africa, either," Marcia said.

Fatts laughed. "We're going to see Pat. She wants to show you the houses women have built for their families."

Pat welcomed us into her home with a warm hug. As we sat in her living room, Sean asked her what drove her to start the housing project.

"It's a long story," Pat said. She originally dreamed of becoming a nurse, but in her final year she got pregnant and had to leave school. After her daughter was born, she worked part-time as a domestic servant and meat hawker in Port Elizabeth.

I felt a certain kinship; we had both lived in the same city.

Later, Pat lobbied the municipality and got them to build a shelter with running water. "It kept the meat fresh." She turned to Sean. "I wanted what many women want—a brick house with a roof and windows that don't leak in the rain—a house with taps so I wouldn't have to line up for water and haul the buckets home."

So in 1992 she invited eight women in her community to start a savings scheme. Each was expected to pay a small amount of money, sometimes very small, every single day towards building their own homes. She named it the Victoria Mxenge Savings Scheme, after the anti-apartheid lawyer who was assassinated in 1985 by government agents. After her death, Victoria Mxenge was awarded the Order of Luthuli in Silver for her "contribution to the struggle for democracy, human rights, nation-building, justice and peace, and conflict resolution."

"The fund just grew and grew," Pat said. When the women had enough money to build, tradesmen showed them what to do. "You should have seen us digging foundations and mixing cement." Pat laughed. "We had to be taught everything. We even learned how to speak to municipal inspectors. My motto was *Ufundu zufes*—we learn until we die."

In 1994 the project became part of the South Africa Homeless People's Federation in Cape Town. From this body, groups could apply for loans or assistance. In a decade the federation grew to over 100,000 members, and by then the women had built thousands of homes. Pat became chair of the federation.

Pat rose to her feet. "Let me show you what the Victoria Mxenge women built." She led us down the streets, pointing out the modest yet sturdy homes. Their first house, erected in 1996 on P Matalongwe

Street., was a "show house" that had cost less than bathroom fittings would have cost in a luxury house in a wealthy Cape Town suburb.

As we walked along, Fatts said, "You know, Pat's achievement was recognized by the UN Secretary-General, Koffi Annan. He presented her with the Humanitarian Award for 1998. It's given to the person who had done the most to alleviate poverty in any country."

Pat gave a wry smile, as if shrugging off the recognition.

On the drive back to the hotel, Sean said, "It's amazing that despite all the odds Pat motivated thousands of families to build their own homes." He was silent for a few moments. "I wish I had her energy and determination."

The return to our former homeland rekindled memories that had dulled over the years, and I longed to bridge the gaps that had arisen in our absence. I called Michael, my friend from law school days. Nearly thirty years had passed, and I was surprised to see that he looked much the same as he had in his youth, except for his increased girth and thinning grey hair. He still had that defining twinkle in his eye and delightful sense of humour. When we exchanged law school memories and quips about our time articling in the same law firm in the 1960s, it seemed as if we had spoken only yesterday.

Michael and Helen Lieberman were no longer the young married couple I remembered, looking to raise a family and build their careers, but two people who had for many years fought to improve the lives of the country's underprivileged.

A speech therapist, in 1963 Helen visited a patient in Langa township and was appalled by the squalor in which the Black community lived. She then regularly and surreptitiously ventured into the township to help the residents. At the time, Whites needed to obtain permits to enter any township, which meant she constantly had to dodge police to avoid arrest. She established a grassroots non-profit organization, Ikamva Labantu (The Future of Our Nation), during the dark days of apartheid.

What started as a small initiative became one of the largest community-based non-profits in South Africa, assisting over a thousand projects to achieve sustainability. Helen served as the president. Ikamva Labantu has established centres for day care, youth and seniors. It addresses the needs of the homeless and people with disabilities, assists rural community development, builds schools and trains teachers, offers sports programs, and runs six job-skills training centres and several factories that employ graduates.

Sean was especially excited to meet Helen. He had read that some people called her the Jewish Mother Theresa for the work she had done.

Helen arranged for us to visit the townships. Sean and Danusia handed out Christmas gifts at the orphanages, laughing with delight at the children's joy and dropping to their knees to hug and tickle them. "The Mamas are amazing," Sean said afterwards. "They love those kids like their own."

Helen then took us to a factory that provided much-needed employment for township women. We watched the women at work, sewing machines whizzing, as they made items for sale. Sean purchased a doll that resembled Nelson Mandela.

We now treasure that doll for what it meant to Sean. Could there be any greater admiration shown to Mandela than for Sean to place the doll in front of him, before his eyes closed for the last time?

As we said goodbye, Helen turned to Sean. "If you want, you can come and stay with Michael and me for a while and work at Ikamva Labantu."

He opened his mouth. Closed it and smiled. "Thank you very much. It's a wonderful offer. I'll definitely think about it."

Back in Toronto, Sean announced one day that he wanted to nominate Helen for CNN Heroes. I agreed it was a wonderful idea and encouraged him to write the letter. Time passed, and on a few more occasions he mentioned nominating her. We offered to help him with the letter, but he never did write it. As is typical of depression, procrastination intervened.

Marcia and I also urged him, a number of times, to accept Helen's generous offer of work and accommodation. Every time he promised to consider it but was never able to commit himself to going.

I wonder if his life would have turned out differently had he embarked on this new direction.

In South Africa we reconnected with Albie Sachs and his wife, Vanessa September. Sean had met them when they stayed with us on a visit to Toronto. Albie, a judge of the Constitutional Court, had taken a stand against the apartheid system that nearly cost him his life.

At their home in Clifton, we sat in the living room and talked about the past, the politics of the present and the concerns facing the country post-apartheid, particularly the vast economic inequality that existed between Black and White people. Sean and Danusia listened with rapt attention.

I mentioned the most unforgettable moment I had experienced in theatre—seeing an excerpt from the *Jail Diary of Albie Sachs* performed in a former church on Bloor Street, in Toronto.

"I would have loved to have seen it," Vanessa said, "but I hadn't met Albie yet."

Albie looked at me, surprised. "You remembered."

Marcia and I had gone to the event in March 1989. The performance space in front of the pews was empty but for a toilet, an incongruous prop inside a church.

A prominent Canadian actor, R.H. Thomson, played the role of Albie, a prisoner in solitary confinement. Albie had been detained in Cape Town under the 90-Day Act, which provided that a person could be detained without trial for ninety days, and could then be rearrested.

Albie had been kept in isolation. The authorities intended to break his resolve not to impart any information to the Security Police.

Each day dragged on.

On the ninetieth day he was handed a document—an order for his release. He was asked to sign a receipt for all his property and told that he could leave. The actor's elation portrayed Albie's taste of freedom.

"You're not going to arrest me again?" the actor asked.

"You are completely free," the officer said.

He asked if he could phone his mother.

The officer agreed. Then, as the actor playing Albie was preparing to leave, the officer strode up to him. "I'm placing you under arrest."

The lights dimmed on R.H. Thomson sitting on the toilet seat. Facing the audience, he said, "Now I'm going to make you sit and stare. You mustn't talk, or read your programs, or look at other people. For two minutes, you must sit and stare."

In the silence and semi-dark, I tried to imagine the sickening shock of facing another ninety days and the strength of will it had taken to remain silent and not incriminate others.

The two minutes felt like twenty.

When the lights gradually brightened, a man in the audience stood up, walked down the aisle and climbed the steps onto the stage. It seemed to me that he was about to intrude right into the performance.

Thomson rose from the toilet seat and unexpectedly hugged him. I saw then that the man had only one arm. He was the real Albie Sachs! He had lost an eye and his right arm in 1988, when he narrowly escaped being assassinated in Maputo by a car bomb planted by agents of the apartheid government.

The audience burst into exuberant applause at this riveting moment of recognition.

We continued our conversation at Clifton Beach. Albie, Sean and I rolled up our trousers and with Danusia and Vanessa strolled along the soft white sand at the water's edge.

Instinctively at one point, I felt for my car keys. Sure enough, my pockets were flat. I worried aloud about contacting Avis, the car rental company, and the logistics of collecting another set of keys.

Albie suggested the obvious, that I might have dropped them. "Let's retrace our steps," he said. We walked back slowly in the setting sun, kicking the sand for buried keys.

No luck.

"I wonder if you left them in the car," Sean said. "I'll run up to see."

"I couldn't have left them in the car," I said, exasperated. "If I did, the car will probably have been stolen by now."

This was exactly the kind of mishap we did not need on vacation.

Minutes later Sean returned, breathless. "The keys were sticking out of the lock in the trunk. You must have left them there when you took out the flowers for Vanessa." He beamed. "It's amazing the car was still there. It was parked at the bus stop and everyone standing there could see the keys."

"This is a story I can repeat," Albie said with a broad smile. "Even with all the crime in South Africa, there are still many honest people here."

A few months after we returned to Toronto, Sean burst into our house, beaming. "Danusia and I are getting engaged!"

Marcia and I were overjoyed. Just seeing Sean walk around with a smile on his face was deeply gratifying.

"Maybe the trip to South Africa cemented their relationship," I said to Marcia later.

Soon after the engagement party at our house, Sean and Danusia started drawing up the guest list for the wedding. He excitedly shared each step of the arrangements with us.

One afternoon he came to the house unshaven. "There are many things we can't agree on," he said softly. "The size of the wedding, the caterers and even whether we're going to live in her apartment or mine. I don't know if it's going to work out."

I asked if the practical concerns could be resolved.

"We'll keep trying," he answered.

After Sean left, Marcia said, "I hope it'll work out, but they both have to deal with their own issues."

A week later Sean broke the news: "Danusia and I are parting. It's just not working out."

There was little we could say.

"Marcia and I like her very much," I said cautiously, "and we feel bad for both of you. At least you had some special times together." I pictured them holding hands, laughing and smiling as they looked into each other's eyes. My memories of their holiday with us were filled with such happy moments.

I knew Marcia and I would one day return to South Africa, but I did not anticipate that we would make the journey in honour of Sean's memory.

SIXTEEN

Please Don't Wear Orange

I steeled myself to open the plastic box containing Sean's private papers—to intrude into his feelings, fears and hopes. I wondered what more I would find.

On top was a notebook with black binding. I flipped through the pages and saw a note addressed to me. It began: "I'm very sorry I pushed to purchase the place that was $185,000 instead of $145,000. I feel awful. I wished I wouldn't have been so impulsive."

The note took me back to the horror of that Passover night when Marcia and I had rushed to the Sherbourne Street overpass—to Sean wavering at the parapet. He told us afterward that he'd been tormented by anxiety, convinced that someone was going to forge his signature and steal his condo.

Now, reading the note, I wondered if his inability to afford the condo on his own was what had truly distressed him. He wanted to finance the condo from the sale of his townhouse, but none of the properties within his price range were suitable.

Sean and I had inspected many apartments. Before we set out, he insisted that the unit have no steps or carpeting, only hardwood floors.

"Why?" I asked.

He hesitated to collect his thoughts. "I expect I'll soon need a wheelchair. My back and ankle are getting worse. There's little the doctors can do about it."

I was shocked at his answer. I knew about his pain. However, I had been hopeful that through his persistence in seeking treatments, he would conquer it or make it more manageable.

The first property he took me to see was a relatively inexpensive one on the sixth floor of a high-rise building. The balcony appeared to be covered in snow, which was odd in the summer heat. I walked out to look and the stench hit my nostrils. "Sean," I burst out, "This isn't snow. It's covered in bird shit."

Next we visited a twelfth-floor apartment. From the balcony I looked down at the tiny cars and people. I worried about Sean living so high up, unable to shake the image of him poised at the parapet of the overpass.

Sean, however, had insisted that we view the apartment.

In the foyer, an elderly woman in a housecoat and slippers shuffled along the worn carpet. I smiled at her and asked what it was like, living in the building.

She looked at me suspiciously. "It's okay when the elevators work. Otherwise, it's hell."

Fortunately, the unit that I helped Sean purchase was on the second floor, in a different building.

What Sean's real fears were that Passover night, I will never know. But his note indicated that he wanted to remedy the condo situation; he was considering selling it or paying me back. I felt heavy-hearted at the possibility that anxiety over accepting money from me had pushed him to the edge.

As I sorted through his things, I realized that his concern for me reflected a larger pattern: an ongoing consideration for family and friends. I would learn more later.

Sean's collection of soft toys was much easier to deal with than his folders, files, medical records, drawings and notebooks. He'd bought them as gifts for nephews and nieces.

The furry animals had quaint names. There was Jungle Joe, the game warden teddy bear in a brown safari outfit, Fuzzles the pink monkey with white spots, Russ puppies with white, brown or black legs. There was the Gund Teddy Bear of The Best Police in his small blue uniform. I rubbed its cute snout against my cheek for a while.

Then I turned to the three-foot-high panda that still sits on a couch in our basement. Sean had bought a similar one for Theo, his nephew. He had also given an enormous brown bear to Michael, the son of our friends Stephen and Susan, when they returned to Cape Town.

After Sean's passing, we were comforted by an email from Michael's father:

Susan and I are thinking about you all day, and we will be seeing Sean tonight when Michael goes to bed. Sean's Big Brown Bear still sits at the bottom of Michael's bed every night, watching over him as he sleeps. We won't be telling him that Sean is gone because, for Michael, he isn't. He is alive with us here, on the other side of the world. So know that he will be held a little closer tonight when the lights go out. And know that when you put your light out, Big Brown Bear will be seeing the sun rise outside his window, shining in on him and his friend, our love forever, Stephen, Susan and Michael.

I gently ran my fingers over the fluffy toys and felt a warm glow suffuse me. I could imagine Sean's joy as he purchased the toys far in advance, then handed them out as gifts to children he loved. Even when his days darkened, his concern and love for them never dimmed.

One diary entry was particularly poignant.

It was dated March 2, 1996. Sean, then twenty, was in first year at Concordia University. He was one of a handful of students accepted into the theatre performance program; the competition for admission was stiff.

Marcia, coincidently, was working at the Open University in London that year. In her absence, I felt more responsible to connect with Sean and often made the six-hour drive to Montreal to visit him. The diary entry revealed his intense appreciation of those visits.

> I spent the day going back to Concordia with my Dad and I had [a] wonderful time … Like I find spending time with him not just glows so well on me, like wow! We had a really nice lunch today. I had fish. Last night I really shared a lot of my experiences with Dad at the Thai restaurant—told him all about my feelings at Concordia, etc., etc. … As I remember back I need a reaction from him! Still, I noticed too as I was ending the trip in the car the same haunting feeling came over me how I am hurt by my father's absence; how he picks up and leaves.

I clasped the diary shut and soaked in the meaning of the words. What a jolt, just absorbing his need to be with me. I felt a mix of appreciation that he wanted to spend more time with me and a hollowed-out sense of regret that it didn't happen more often.

Sean had become fascinated with the world of theatre during high school. Marcia was teaching theatre at York University, and Sean helped her prepare Power Point presentations and converted plays from video into a format she could use in the classroom.

He often engaged Marcia in discussions of her work and sought out her opinions about the transformative nature of theatre. On occasion, I joined in. She had a way of looking at situations from a different perspective. In this and other ways, she led us into a world that otherwise we never would have encountered. "Why do you teach such tough plays?" Sean asked. "They all deal with heavy topics—rape, torture, arrest, sexual-harassment, stalking, racism, homophobia."

Marcia explained that at her age, in her late forties, she felt strongly about raising issues that would shake students out of their complacency and encourage them to connect with problems in their own surroundings.

One night near the end of term, Sean called me from Montreal.

"I can't study here anymore. Please come and fetch me as soon as possible."

"Don't you want to finish the year? It's only a few weeks to go."

He insisted he could not go on. He sounded desperate.

I drove to Montreal early the following morning. When I got there, Sean hadn't finished packing and clearing his room. I watched him sweep the floor until it was spotless. He then folded his bedding and returned crockery and cutlery to the kitchen.

"I have to say goodbye to a few of my friends," he said. "They won't know what happened if I just disappeared. I don't want them to worry."

I waited for nearly an hour.

"Sorry it took so long," he said. "I said goodbye to my friends and had to find the housekeeper and waiters who were nice to me, to thank them and say goodbye."

When Sean took his own life, he did not say goodbye. I know he had tried to be considerate in the manner of his leaving. He couldn't have imagined how his death would devastate our lives.

The preparations for his final leaving were meticulous: the computer printout describing the method of ending his life, the unlocked cell phone, the gas receipt, the credit cards, the bottles of medication neatly set out, not to mention all his stored documents, photos, drawings, medical records, and notebooks. And yet he did not say goodbye, knowing we would have tried to stop him and he'd be prevented from following through on his plans to take his life.

As we were driving back to Toronto, Sean thanked me for coming to fetch him without trying to persuade him to finish the year. "You probably want to know why I wanted to leave suddenly." I nodded. He explained that the instructor of his small acting class was behaving strangely. He and the other students thought she might have mental health issues. The personal interaction required in the group made it unbearable for him and some others to continue to attend.

"I really do appreciate your coming," he said again. "A classmate of mine wanted to leave, but his parents insisted he complete the term. My friend couldn't continue. He attempted suicide, and ended up in hospital in a vegetative state."

I was so thankful that I had listened and gone to Montreal to bring him home.

Years later, shortly after Sean's death, we met a friend of his from Concordia. "I must tell you something you probably don't know," she said. "Near the end of the academic year Sean suddenly gave away nearly all his clothes. I was shocked and asked him why he did so. All he would say was that he had too much 'stuff.'"

This information appalled me. Was he already contemplating suicide?

Among the files in the plastic container was a brown folder with *God I Hope This Pain Will Go Away* scribbled on the tab. I had picked it up and put it back a few times, afraid to open it.

Sean had often mentioned his persistent lower back, neck and ankle pain. The first report in the folder was from a chiropractor whom he had consulted when he turned thirty. He was advised to wear custom orthotics to alleviate the symptoms. Unfortunately, that did not seem to help.

The following year Sean sought help from Bridgepoint Hospital in Toronto, enrolling in their ten-week pain management course. According to the hospital's website, the program "uses a cognitive-behavioural approach and physical activity to provide coping strategies. It is available to people with a medically stable chronic pain condition, which has been present for longer than six months and not been responsive to traditional medical intervention." This seemed to apply to Sean.

In his final report, the physician noted that while punctuality was sometimes an issue for Sean, he commended him for attending all the scheduled twenty sessions, the only one in the group to do so. Sean had saved the Certificate of Accomplishment.

The physician wrote further:

Sean also emphasized the education, which helped him understand more about the connection between pain and mood, the value of rest, the importance that attitudes play in coping with the pain and he is now able to engage more with pain rather than denying it and is less dependent on the opinions of others. Further goals include continuing to apply to pain clinics for further understanding about his pain and any medical treatments that might be available.

At the time, Sean didn't share the report with me, but we often talked about his persistent pain and the inability to find a physical cause. He acknowledged, once, that his pain could be psychosomatic. It couldn't be explained by medical tests or physical examinations.

In addition to meeting with his psychiatrist, he consulted with a sports medicine physician, attended physiotherapy and acupuncture sessions, and practiced meditation.

The last report I read was from a radiologist. Sean was suffering from pain in both hands and wrists. The report stated, "No fracture or dislocation is apparent. Joint spaces are preserved, and there is no peri-articular erosion or other findings to suggest arthritis."

I slowly closed the folder, overwhelmed by a mixture of emotions: admiration for Sean's tenacity and persistence as he struggled to alleviate his enduring pain, frustration at our limited understanding of how what arises in the mind is reflected in the body, and sorrow. Having tried everything, Sean eventually lost all hope.

Sean's three older brothers each had a special place in their hearts for their kid brother. They often reached out, inviting him to social gatherings, movies and concerts, all the more so when it became clear that he was suffering.

When Sean left home the first time, he went to stay with Jonathan on Dundas Street, near Bathurst. They attended concerts together, and because of the location, Sean was able to enjoy the city's bustling downtown core.

After he left Concordia he enrolled at York University and graduated with a degree in psychology. Uncertain on a career choice, he debated with each member of the family about what he should do next.

Kevin arranged employment for Sean at the internet service company where he was working. At age fifteen, Kevin had helped create the technology for the company with one of Toronto's internet pioneers, Allan Park. Allan had foreseen the vast potential of the internet. He called his company The Wire. Kevin left the company on being appointed Vice-President of New Technologies at a technology company headquartered in Boulder, Colorado.

One night Sean said, "The Wire won't last. The dial-up system is becoming outdated and the company's losing money every month."

When I mentioned that to Jonathan, who had also joined The Wire, he said, "Sean is like the canary in a coal mine."

I negotiated with Allan to purchase the company. I bought it on blind faith, hoping that Kevin's return to The Wire would put it right. Fortunately, it did, which in turn justified our confidence in Kevin's ability.

After a few years, when work at The Wire became too exacting, Sean asked to join my law office to do legal research. He often spoke to me about becoming a lawyer, and started preparing for the Law School Admission Test (LSAT).

Sean obtained all his university transcripts for entrance to Osgoode Hall Law School and with advice from Marcia, Mark and me prepared the forms. In one of his answers he referred to his degree in psychology and wrote that his health psychology professor was so impressed with an experiment he had devised on sleep patterns that she asked to use it as a model for students to consult in the reserve library. I now understand better his particular interest in sleep patterns, recalling the irregular times he retired at night and his difficulty arising in the morning

He completed the application form, questioning all the while if he was making the right decision, while we provided reassurance.

However, even the best crafted application cannot be accepted if it is never submitted.

I was happy to see him at the office. At the same time, I was perturbed by how often he closed his door and detached himself from his surroundings for many hours.

Mentally, Sean kept withdrawing into another space. After two years in my office, he decided he was no longer interested in being a lawyer. More concerning was his lack of interest in pursuing a career path of any kind.

When Mark as a teenager got a newspaper route, Sean became his regular helper. Many years later, Mark graduated as a lawyer and specialized in charity law. He involved Sean in creating a large online database of non-profit entities as a public service to provide donors with greater clarity in making their funding choices. Mark later named the database the *Sean Blumberg Transparency Project* in memory of Sean.

His brothers continued to reach out to him, but as his depression deepened, he declined most invitations.

One night, seven years after Sean passed away, Jonathan came over, wanting to talk with Marcia and me. As we sat in our family room, sipping coffee, Jonathan said, "There's a missing link, something we should have tried."

"What do you mean?" I believed that Sean had exhausted every avenue to deal with his mental health issues and that Marcia and I had done all we could to help him in his distress.

"Did anyone ever suggest to you early on, when Sean started

having a difficult time, that we should try a family intervention?"

We shook our heads, not understanding what he meant.

Jonathan explained that in their childhood and teens all the siblings had bonded, as expected of four brothers. He had taken Sean under his wing, and Mark did the same for Kevin. "We all had special relationships. Maybe in his late teens and early twenties, when things started going badly, he would have been open to the family gathering around him in a supportive way."

By his late twenties, Sean had withdrawn. Jonathan recalled approaching him in his usual friendly manner at a family dinner to give him a big hug. Sean moved away quickly, saying his back hurt.

"I wish I'd understood what was happening to him," Jonathan said. "You and Mom tried to explain what was going on, but somehow, looking back, I feel that Mark, Kevin, and I were mostly in the dark. Input from us might have helped."

"What more could you all have done?" Marcia asked.

"We could have brainstormed ideas—maybe Sean going to a different city or country would have put him in a different space. Who knows? However, we were never provided with any opportunity for input."

I began to understand that Jonathan not only suffered grief at Sean's passing but self-reproach that he hadn't raised the possibility of an intervention at the time.

In Sean's teens and his early twenties, Marcia and I were unaware of the extent of the significant changes taking place in his life. He shared very little with us during those years. When we read the Facebook entries about him, we were delighted and surprised to discover the many meaningful friendships he once had and his passion for sports and music. He did tell us about going to art therapy and counselling, but we only realized much later the depth of his despair. By then it was too late for a worthwhile family intervention.

I recalled how we pleaded, cajoled and urged Sean to see a psychiatrist. That seemed to be working out, but one day Sean said, "Dad, I like him. He's very caring, but after four years I'm getting nowhere.

I need to see someone else." Sean summed up his three visits to his next psychiatrist by saying, "He seemed to feel that I was in a privileged position and should get on with things." Over many months we followed up on further referrals that didn't work out. Eventually, we were successful in connecting Sean with his last psychiatrist.

If Sean's professional caregivers had suggested a family intervention, Sean never mentioned it to us. I wondered aloud why they hadn't approached us directly.

"There's a professional comfort zone that can be exclusionary of parents and siblings," Jonathan said. "Perhaps they were concerned about privacy issues, or Sean was adamantly against the idea."

Maybe it was the "missing link." We will never know.

One afternoon, a few years before Sean took his life, Marcia received a phone call from Sean's psychiatrist. She touched the speaker button so that I could hear. "Sean is here with me and asked me to call you. I know it sounds strange, but he would really appreciate it if you did not wear orange-coloured clothing anymore."

Marcia looked startled. "Why?"

"Sean will tell you more later."

I knew from watching television that prisoners often wore orange jumpsuits, but I couldn't understand how that related to Sean.

When he came over to the house that night for dinner, he walked slowly and seemed to be in pain. He told us that he was worried that he could be charged by the police. I was shocked at his statement. At first he was reluctant to say more. After much persistence on my part, he explained his concern.

"You know Jackie?"

He had once introduced Jackie to Marcia and me. A thin woman with dishevelled, ginger-brown hair, she had said very little. Sean had befriended her at a group therapy session. She'd had an argument with her adoptive parents, and they had asked her to move out. He felt sorry for her and offered the spare room in his apartment while she sorted out her life.

Sean spoke quickly as if he wanted to unburden himself of the story. “For a few months it all worked out well. My back and neck had been giving me real problems and I had difficulty doing my shopping. The deal was that she would do the shopping and help with chores.”

Jackie had a friend, he told us, who came over regularly, and that was fine. However, the number of her visitors increased to three and at times four, each carrying a pack of beer. He described one as a hulking brute. They raised their voices and swigged their beer, comfortably ensconced in his armchairs till late at night. Feeling vulnerable for his safety and afraid of arousing their anger, he was hesitant to ask them to leave. Finally, a neighbour banged for silence on the adjoining wall.

“You guys should go now,” Sean said.

They didn’t move. They just stared at him. “I had to ask them a few more times. I was afraid the neighbour would bang on the wall again. Eventually they left, but they made me feel very uncomfortable in the process.”

After that incident, Sean told Jackie to meet her friends elsewhere. She just laughed at him. And she stopped helping with the shopping and chores.

He looking down. “It got much worse with her. So I had to ask her to move out. She became very angry and threatened to get back at me.”

“What did she mean by that?” I asked.

“Well, she could get her friends to attack me. She could even lay some criminal charge against me with the police for assaulting her—or something much worse.”

“Do you really think they would believe her? They’d see it was all a lie, a ridiculous story.” I stopped myself from asking what he meant by “something much worse.”

He looked down at the carpet and paused for a while. “She just has to get a bruise somewhere and concoct enough of a story with her friends to get me into trouble or even jail."

I shuddered at the thought of all the consequences.

Sean turned to Marcia. "I know you love the colour orange. Even if I never hear from her again, I don't want to be reminded of what could or might still happen. So please don't wear orange."

A few days later Sean told us that Jackie had calmed down. He helped her find alternative accommodation, paid her initial rent and made all the arrangements for her move.

Many months later I asked him if he had heard from her. He shook his head.

But the embers of fear she had instilled in him still flickered, bursting now and again into a flame of paranoia.

Marcia never again wore orange.

SEVENTEEN

Sean Left Quietly

One evening a couple of weeks after Sean's funeral, a friend from his teenage years phoned and asked to visit his grave. Lucky Budd had moved to Vancouver and was in Toronto for a few days. The call was unexpected but much appreciated.

Lucky and many other friends who had known Sean before he withdrew into his closed world had posted heart-warming condolences on Facebook. They remembered a vibrant, mischievous, inquisitive Sean, a teenager passionate about music, sports, and the arts. Their insights helped us to recover who Sean was before his light was overshadowed by depression, anxiety, and most of all, paranoia—which had been heightened by the threatening behaviour of his so-called friend, Jackie.

Even though Lucky had not seen Sean for more than ten years, he wrote of Sean's sensitivity, honesty, and profound influence on his life. It hadn't been a secret to him that Sean had been suffering for a long time. Directed to Sean he wrote, "I am so sorry you couldn't reconnect with that amazing kid inside of you again. As sad as I am for your family and myself, I am happy for you that your suffering has ended."

He recalled Sean's love of sport, the many road hockey games they played, and the memorable night they were together in 1992 when the Blue Jays won their first World Series and all of Canada erupted in spontaneous exultation. Even though I hadn't followed the series, I could not but be swept up, as a Canadian, in the contagion of joy.

I drove Lucky, Jonathan and Marcia to the Pardes Shalom Cemetery the next morning in Marcia's Acura TL, the car that Sean had loved to drive.

Lucky began to open up. "Sean meant a lot to me. He was one of the best people I ever knew. Thank you for this opportunity to say goodbye."

Grass had yet to grow over the scarred brown soil, and the flowers strewn on the grave lay faded and withered. A small plastic plaque fixed to a silvery spike had been placed by the undertakers, Benjamin's Park Memorial Chapel, to mark Sean's burial site. The inscription said, "Sean Blumberg. August 26, 2012 - 8 Elul 5772" and "Forever In Our Hearts." Someone had stuck a sunflower in the spike. It was a fitting symbol: the stalk cut short, the outer circle of bright yellow florets evoking the joyous years of Sean's life, the dark disc at the centre, the internal darkness that enveloped him.

Lucky, dressed in a long-sleeved striped cream shirt that hung over his blue jeans, gently placed his yellow guitar case on the grass next to the grave and scattered fresh flowers on the soil. He stood in silence gazing at the site for a few minutes. Then he pushed his dark sunglasses over his black hair and started talking about his relationship with Sean when they were teenagers.

As a parent, I was never fully aware of our teenagers' escapades or even their whereabouts. Yes, we exchanged thoughts, hopes and disappointments, and enjoyed meals, family holidays and celebrations together, but there would always be a gap between what Marcia and I knew and the reality of our sons' worlds. That was the nature of parenting teenagers. Now I yearned to discover more about Sean's teenage years. My hope was that Lucky would help me fill that gap.

Sean, he said, had been his best friend between the ages of twelve and sixteen. During those vital, formative years, Sean had been his soul mate, that pivotal, first like-minded friend. "Sean was always decisive. He gave me the courage to feel secure in myself and express who I really was." Lucky shook his head. "Back then, when we imagined who was going to have a successful life, no one thought that Sean would just ..."

Lucky spoke of their teenage escapades. How they skipped school to go and see the Blue Jays play at 1:30. "Sean would say, 'I'll leave after lunch and meet you on the bus.' That was the sort of thing we did."

His voice grew animated, as if he were channelling Sean's vibrancy. "Sean organized football games on Sunday afternoons. He was the one who brought us together and made it all happen."

I listened, mesmerized. I knew Sean loved playing sports, but I was unaware that he revelled in being at the centre of it all. I was even more surprised and delighted to hear Sean described as decisive. To me he had appeared tentative, as if asking for permission to do anything.

I pictured Sean's shoulder-length hair and irrepressible energy. Many years later we realized that this lengthy period of hyperactivity was the first sign of his bipolar condition.

I was moved when Lucky mentioned how proud Sean was of all of us; Marcia was studying and following a path towards a PhD, and Sean gleaned interesting ideas from our family's talks.

As Lucky spoke, I gazed at the rows of tombstones. On every marble or granite slab, people had placed stones—large ones, small ones, round, angular, rough, smooth. There were many explanations for this tradition. Some said it was to show that a mourner had come to visit the grave. Others thought the stones anchored the souls where they belonged; to me, that felt uncomfortably like eternal imprisonment. I believe the stones symbolize the permanence of the soul, just as flowers signify the beauty, but also the fragility and brevity, of life.

Despite the close friendship between Sean and Lucky, they only attended the same high school, York Mills Collegiate, for two months. One of Sean's teachers told Marcia, "Sean is the naughtiest child I've ever taught. He is very, very bright. But something is not right. You should go and have him tested."

Tests confirmed that he was "naughty," thanks to sheer boredom.

Sean's placement in the gifted program at Earl Haig Secondary School seemed the right move at the time. "You know, Dad," Sean said, "they don't repeat the same sentence six times here."

In their late teens, Lucky noticed a change in his friend. Sean appeared downcast, less exuberant. He went out less and seldom smiled.

The last time he saw Sean, Lucky said, was in 1996, after first-year university. By then Sean's other school friends had lost contact with him; they had no idea what was happening to him.

As I reflect on Lucky's words, I am reminded of a firefly's glow and the trail of darkness it leaves behind as its light fades and disappears.

I remembered how Sean had retreated to his room. He did not want his friends to know about his struggles. Marcia and I didn't mention his concerns to anybody other than family members and a few of our close friends who cared and asked. At the time Marcia said that she felt as if she was living a double life. Outwardly, she was the professional academic and grandmother with a charming smile, while inside she was in deep distress.

I was slower to appreciate the toll all that was taking on me. Only after Sean passed away did I fully realize my own chronic anguish, the constant anxiety I had felt all that time.

Lucky picked up his guitar. In a low voice, he said that before Sean's funeral he envisioned a scene where Sean stood in front of him and spoke in a casual tone. "You know, Lucky, nobody expects you to come right now. Why don't you come out in a couple of weeks? Grab your guitar and go out to the grave and sing a song and say goodbye."

He sat down cross-legged on the grass next to the fresh grave and began strumming. "Sean knew exactly what song I was going to play—'Brokedown Palace' by the Grateful Dead."

Jonathan hummed quietly while Lucky sang.

The lyrics remind me now of the sapling we planted in our garden in Sean's memory. As the years passed, Marcia and I trimmed and nourished it, watched it thrive. It grew higher and higher and reached for the sky. Glistening with icicles in winter and cloaked in greenery in summer, the tree burst into vibrant orange in the fall—reminding me of Sean's request that Marcia not wear orange.

The change of seasons, like the tree, evoked memories of happy and difficult times in Sean's life.

In the quiet time that followed after all the shiva guests had left, Marcia and I read and reread the bereavement cards and Facebook entries of friends from Sean's teenage years.

Brendan, a friend at Concordia University, wrote that Sean was an "inspiration" to him. His "penetrating intelligence and deep sensitivity" had awakened his own "curiosity and creativity." Oh, how I missed those aspects of Sean.

His former fiancé, Danusia, encapsulated much about him in one paragraph. The words "funny, witty, bright, gentle, caring," resonated with me. Despite the ending of their engagement, she graciously added, "I feel truly blessed to have shared time and space with this special man."

Some of the postings provided insights into Sean's life and loves that Marcia and I had not been aware of. Athena shared her remembrances from twenty years before of Sean being her best friend and lover; they talked for hours about philosophy, dreams, and the world. I wondered why he had never discussed philosophy with me; it was one of my majors. Maybe I'd been remiss in not opening the door to such discussions.

Anna described wonderful memories of their love and exceptional relationship. She wrote of their camping trip to Quebec. He organized everything. She recalled how they biked fast down a wild nature trail and stopped by a waterfall. "We took pictures, you were thin, and strong, and smiling so sweetly, in a green t-shirt and shorts, hair pulled back in a ponytail. At some point on that trip we danced, by water I think—the way you were when you were younger was so full of energy and light it was like you floated, you were that light."

She still cherished his art. "All reds and yellows and orange, like a flame on paper, burning as bright as you did. You were incredibly creative and fun and unstoppable. We couldn't then have imagined how different circumstances would become."

When she went to Paris on a babysitting trip, Sean insisted that she make the most of it by travelling around Europe. However, she missed him too much. She came home early to spend a few weeks with him before leaving for university in Montreal. Sean was staying behind to finish his last year at Earl Haig. She didn't want to miss the short time left to be with him.

We received many more comforting and beautiful expressions of condolence and memories from Sean's friends. How we treasured these messages! They shone a light on his joyous spirit during those short but memorable years.

One evening Marcia wondered aloud whether Sean's friends would continue to write messages on his Facebook page as the years passed. I thought it unlikely; his friends would move on with their own lives as they married, raised families and pursued their careers.

I was grateful to be proven wrong.

The following year, on the first anniversary of his death, we were touched to read postings from Sean's friends from his teenage years. Many continued to share beautiful recollections every year.

Jonathan echoed the feelings of everyone in our family when he wrote of missing Sean and wishing that they had had more time together. Many working parents, in retrospect, face the sudden truth that their children have grown up and sealed themselves into their own private space. The remorse is even worse when the child or sibling is no longer with us.

Jonathan had taken over Sean's car. On the long drive from our cottage down Highway 11 and the 400 to Toronto, the wonky gas meter indicated that the tank was filling up. Normally, it would just stick. It was as if the tank was expanding, Jonathan wrote, under the pressure of memories, wishes and dreams.

The next year he wrote of the elephant key ring on the dashboard. It reminded him of Sean's big presence and huge absence. I, too, had kept many of Sean's possessions. I resisted parting with anything as memories flooded back.

Many of his friends wrote on his birthdays. Suja wished him happy birthday and added, "You are with us all." In thinking of him she could at times not breathe. We had kept in touch with her since the funeral. I can imagine Sean smiling and saying, "Thank you for reaching out to her. I couldn't tell her what I was going to do. So thank you."

Pauline, a cousin in Los Angeles, wrote, "I look at Sean's picture all the time and think about how precious he is." When I visited her, I was touched to see a photo of our family displayed in her living room.

Rosslyn wrote from South Africa. We had not been in contact since we left Port Elizabeth thirty-three years ago. I felt the poignancy of her message: "How hard it is to move on … you have to move on." I remembered the tragic loss of their son, Jonathan's childhood friend, coincidentally also called Sean.

Messages have been posted every year, some on his birthday, and others on the date of his death, keeping his memory alive.

In 2019, on the seventh anniversary of Sean's death, Jonathan wrote that he was looking forward to a road trip with me along the Blues Trail from Memphis to New Orleans. That October, as we drove that iconic highway, we listened, hummed, and mouthed the tunes on Sean's treasured cassette tapes: *Led Zeppelin IV*, *Best of the*

Guess Who and Clapton, Dark Side of Moon, Abbey Road, The Joshua Tree, and *American Beauty*. The haunting lyrics of "Brokedown Palace" evoked the wrench of parting from one's beloved.

I thought of Sean and the difference he made to many lives. What more can any person hope to achieve?

I heard Marcia whisper, "Seanie, please look after Henry."

The hulking orderly hovered over me, ready to wheel me on the narrow gurney down the hallway. I felt an acute tingle of hyperawareness, as if being pushed into a dark tunnel. I prayed that I would come out on the other side into the light.

I knew what Marcia meant. At the start and end of each day, she would look at the photo of Sean on the computer screen, share her thoughts with him, pray that he was at peace and not alone in whatever universe he had reached. It was part of her ritual of remembering Sean and helped to assuage her grief.

I had gone for my annual medical checkup a few months before Sean passed away. At the time I felt fine, but when my family doctor pressed his stethoscope to my chest, he said, "You've got a heart murmur. I'll send you to a cardiologist. It's probably nothing. Chances are, you were born with it." He had first heard the murmur years before after a stress test, and he said it wasn't serious.

I was unconcerned. Three months after Sean passed away, I still resisted seeing the cardiologist, as I continued to feel well. I only reluctantly made the appointment because Marcia kept reminding me about it, as a caring spouse would do.

This time, when the cardiologist placed his stethoscope on my chest, what I heard was new. "Aortic valve stenosis, you need a new valve. Valve's tight. It's quite common between seventy-five and eighty. You'll probably need a bypass as well."

I was amazed at his diagnosis. I thought I was *fine*. How strange. I smiled inwardly, wondering if he was short of business. Yet his waiting room was filled with patients.

"One day," he said, "you will thank me for saving your life."

The seriousness of my condition sank in. Then came the tests. An echocardiogram and an angiogram showed a constriction. I would need a new valve and a double bypass.

The surgery at Toronto General Hospital took place November 30, 2012, exactly three months after Sean's funeral.

The operation took longer than expected. Mark, Kevin, Jonathan and his wife, Pam, took turns sitting with Marcia in the waiting room. The surgeon had promised that a nurse would report on my progress.

Marcia said later, "We got worried when no nurse appeared." She stopped for a few seconds, upset at reliving the experience.

Marcia went to the receptionist and asked why the operation was taking so long. After a while, an anxious-looking nurse rushed out.

"Things are okay now," she said, and hurried back to the operating theatre.

Marcia later told me that the surgeon, when he appeared in his green surgical gown, said, "His condition was much worse than I thought. It's okay now. He only had a month, maybe two, left. Lucky he didn't wait any longer."

There is nothing like a near-death experience to bring home the icy realization of one's mortality.

Mark was shocked when he saw me lying in the intensive care unit, hooked up to tubes and buzzing and blinking monitors. "Henry looked worse than Sean afterwards," he told Marcia.

Of course, I didn't hear what Mark said. What I did hear was what Marcia told me later as she held my hand. "Sean must have interceded."

Eight months after Sean's death, on May 5, 2013, his tombstone at Pardes Shalom Cemetery was unveiled.

A white sheet was draped over the stone. The rabbi pulled it aside, revealing the *Magen Dovid,* sign of David, engraved in the deep green granite. The head of the stone had deliberately been left rough and jagged to evoke an unfinished life. On the back, three words: "He Left Quietly." The phrase is the title of a play about a political prisoner in South Africa, condemned to death during apartheid. In the early morning, the warden comes to the cell to escort the prisoner to the death chamber. "He left quietly," the text says, taking great care not to wake his fellow prisoners, wanting to avoid the tearful goodbyes. With the permission of the playwright, Yael Farber, we inscribed those words—so true of Sean—on the back of the tombstone.

Engraved on the front were the words, "Cherished Brother, Brother-In-Law, Devoted Uncle, Adored Godson, Treasured Friend." And "Dearly Beloved Son of Henry and Marcia." Someday, when we lie near Sean, visitors to the cemetery will see he was our son. The last line chosen for the epitaph expressed our collective feelings: "A Kind, Gentle and Thoughtful Soul. Forever in Our Hearts."

It meant a great deal to us that Rabbi Bielfeld officiated. For over thirty years he had celebrated not only our *simchas*, our happy occasions, he was also there when we needed him even more—for our bereavements. We were concerned that he would not be with us, as that weekend the Governor General was presenting him with the Order of Canada for his humanitarian work. However, true to form, he arose at 3 a.m. on Sunday morning to take the first flight from Ottawa to Toronto.

Marcia had given the eulogy for Sean at the funeral but said she would be too emotional to speak at the unveiling.

Eight months after the death, I felt that I could speak. I read some of the emails we had received. One was from our friend Fatima Dike, the South African Xhosa playwright, who loved and understood Sean. She addressed him:

Sean, I find myself at a loss for words, which is unusual for me. I think this is because the Blumbergs are my family and whatever happens to them happens to me. I want your spirit to move smoothly and I want you to go and be with Grandpa and all the Blumberg ancestors. You deserve it, because you were the gentlest, most caring being I have ever met. From time to time when we come together as family, you will be part of our conversations, you will never be forgotten. Sleep, my brother sleep, you deserve to. In time we'll heal, our hearts will always remember you. I thank you for your presence in my life and in our lives. *Hamba kakuhle kroti lam*, go well my hero, *hamba kakuhle sithandwa sam,* go well my heart. *Lala kakuhle mntanomble,* sleep beautiful child.

She enfolded Sean in the arms of her Xhosa culture, embracing him as a member of her family. Her invocation of Xhosa salutations, reached into the deep chambers of our hearts.

Much of what happened next at the unveiling was a blur. We played Leonard Cohen's soulful song, "Who by Fire." It was his version of an ancient Hebrew liturgical poem. Every year thereafter, on Yom Kippur, the Day of Atonement, I think of Sean as I stand among our congregation with my prayer shawl wrapped around me and listen as the cantor chants the ways of dying: "Who shall live and who shall die; who shall live out his allotted time and who shall depart before his time." The haunting words reverberate within me long after the service.

The unveiling of the tombstone was another part of the passage we had to navigate in remembering and grieving, and in healing. Pain was a constant in our lives, ebbing and flowing like the tide. It would recede for a while, only to rise again.

We, as a family, felt a burning need to keep our memories of Sean alive. Marcia and I found many ways to do so.

Every year our family gathers for a dinner to honour Sean's birthday. Marcia buys his favourite ice cream cake decorated with icing balloons in red, yellow, green and blue.

On one birthday, the inscription on the cake said, *"Beloved Sean—Always in Our Hearts."*

The cashier smiled. "What wonderful words for his birthday."

"Yes. We always want to remember him," Marcia said slowly.

"I'm so sorry," the cashier said, looking down.

Later, our eight grandchildren gathered around, tussling for a balloon their favourite colour. Marcia looked at them lovingly, as only a grandmother can.

"What do you remember about Sean?" she asked before slicing the cake.

Evie, Jonathan and Pam's youngest daughter, said, "I love Sean."

Mia, her older sister said, "Sean was kind."

Kate leaned forward. "He made me laugh."

Theo looked down and didn't answer. His expression showed he felt the loss but preferred to remain silent.

Matthew mentioned that he had long conversations with Sean.

"He was my best hockey fan," Ethan remembered.

Julian, then five years old, hesitated before asking, "Where does Sean sleep?"

"Up there in heaven," Marcia answered.

"No. Where? In what room?"

"He's everywhere, but mostly in our hearts," I answered.

Julian smiled.

Somehow, I believe Sean knows what is happening and how deeply he is missed.

Our family also honours Sean on the anniversary of his death. Every year we light the *yahrzeit* candle, the memorial candle, in his memory. Then I recite the *El Maleh Rachamim*, the Jewish prayer for the dead. The prayer resonates with me as a plea for Sean to be at peace in his resting place and for his soul to be bound among the living. That is what I pray for Sean.

Our friends and family phone, write cards or send emails expressing sympathy. Each year, without fail, our friend Sonita sends a certificate from the Jewish National Fund of Canada recording her purchase of a section of trees planted in Israel in loving memory of Sean.

Our family recollections and rituals, and the kindness of many of Sean's friends, have sustained us. They have become part of our healing process, blunting the anguish that surfaces with every anniversary.

Death begets its own rituals that give comfort to the bereaved.

We regularly visit Sean's grave at the Pardes Shalom Cemetery. We slowly read the inscriptions and feel the ache in our chests as we linger over the words, "*He left quietly.*" On top of the tombstone, among other stones placed there, we added our own in our age-old tradition.

Among the stones we wedged a small inukshuk. We hoped it would guide Sean, wherever he might be, towards the peace that had eluded him. Maybe it would also point those of us who feel his loss so keenly to a path that might lessen our grief.

Close by Sean's grave, we visit that of our granddaughter, Sasha, as we have done so many times before. We add to the stones atop her tombstone. We again read the inscription and gaze at the engraving of her favourite doll, a small Raggedy Ann, and remember how she cuddled it close to her.

Every visit to the cemetery follows a practice of honouring the children of friends. We find the graves of Lisa and Jo-Anne, the twin daughters of our friend, Carmella. We pay our respects, placing stones on their headstones. She does the same for Sean and Sasha's graves whenever she visits and mourns her two daughters. We celebrated their birth in Port Elizabeth, South Africa, more than fifty years ago, never expecting that they would be buried near our son and granddaughter.

Before we leave we return to Sean's grave and once more dwell on the words: "*A kind, thoughtful and gentle soul. Forever in our hearts.*"

All these rites of remembering and the recollections of Sean's childhood and teenage friends have informed us about Sean's life, eased our grief, and helped keep Sean's memory alive.

Sean will continue to live on in our hearts and minds through all of our cherished remembrances.

No one is truly dead until all the memories of him have faded away.

EIGHTEEN

Random Reawakenings

Random happenings surfaced quietly, unannounced, arousing the simmering pain of our loss yet also kindling warm recollections.

A few weeks after the unveiling, Marcia and I had dinner at Glow, a restaurant in the Don Mills Shopping Centre near our house. A server approached our table and smiled. "You were here before, at that table over there." He pointed to the far side of the restaurant. "Yes, you were with a young man in a grey sweater."

I fell speechless. Sean had joined us for dinner and sat opposite Marcia and me. He had worn the tattered grey sweater Katie had often teased him about.

Marcia looked at me to answer.

"What a great memory," I said, struggling for words.

"I take fish oil. It's good for memory." The waiter laughed.

"What's your name?"

"Sean," he said.

Marcia and I stared at each other in disbelief. I couldn't utter the words, *He passed away*. The server must have wondered at my sudden silence. He couldn't have guessed that his casual comment touched a wound that wouldn't heal.

His tip was far greater than he could have expected.

The same tiny fingers that devoured the chocolate ice cream cake at our annual birthday celebrations for Sean also magically delved into forgotten corners and compartments in our house. Once, when Kate was visiting, she came running up to Marcia and me in the family room. "Look what I found." In her hands was a picture of Sean.

Kate had been exploring the antique music desk we had brought from South Africa. Some items are purchased because they are needed, others because they are wanted. This piece of furniture fell into the latter category. The desk was purely ornamental. We hadn't opened its lid in years.

"Is there anything else in the desk?" I asked.

Kate rushed out and came back with two pieces of paper. On one strip was a typed quote of Barack Obama.

that fundamental belief - I am my brother's keeper, I am my sister's keeper - that makes this country work."
— Barack Obama

The word "keeper" resonated deeply and reflected Sean's concern for others: a trait that became more pronounced over the years.

The other note said, "*Don't throw out*," dated March 5, 1988.

Sean was then eleven years old. I held the note and gazed at the words and drawing for a while, unable to speak. We never forsook him and hoped that he had come to realize that.

Kate asked in a broken voice, "Why did he throw himself out?"

Her question was poignant, especially for a nine-year-old. All I could say was that he was really not well.

I sensed his presence as I walked around the house and garden.

"No, he's not there," I repeated to myself.

There were times I went to speak to him about his pain, only to realize that I could not. I would drift between the state of knowing what had happened and incomprehension, unable to confront the reality that he was no longer with us as before.

I yearned for a bridge between reality and imagination as reflected in Joan Didion's memoir. *The Year of Magical Thinking* dealt with the death of her husband from a heart attack, followed by losing her daughter from toxic shock. Didion hoped that by magical thinking, she could make her husband reappear.

Marcia and I had seen the play based on the memoir, starring Vanessa Redgrave, in London in 2008. Now, four years later, we were struggling to fathom the significance of our own loss.

Jonathan asked if he could take a few of Sean's tapes to play as he headed north to our cottage in Muskoka.

"I particularly want to listen to the one by the Grateful Dead about Casey Jones."

"Of course," I said, happy that he shared Sean's choice of music. I thought of my father often bursting into "The Ballad of Casey Jones" as he drove his black Chevy along the corrugated roads near Hoopstad, my original home town in South Africa. Casey Jones became a folk legend when on April 30, 1900, as the engineer on the Cannon Ball Express from Chicago to New Orleans, he saved the lives of his many passengers by avoiding a collision with a freight train.

"You know it was your Grandfather Julius's favourite song. He learnt it as a young man in his twenties when he was working in Greenville, Mississippi."

"When was that?"

"Over a hundred years ago."

I started singing the lyrics out of tune as my father had sung them near the beginning of the last century.

> He looked at his water and his water was low
> He looked at his watch and his watch was slow
> He turned to his fireman and this is what he said
> "Boy, we're going to reach Frisco, but we'll all be dead"

Jonathan laughed. "It's amazing that this song has been sung by four generations in our family."

We looked at each other. I felt the power of the lyrics that crossed from Sean's great-grandfather to him.

In the past, I seldom dreamt. When I did, whatever messages bubbled to the surface fizzled away. Now I dream often and the details linger as I seek to unravel their meaning. Some dreams unlock the gates to the dark chambers of buried feelings; others flood my mind like shadows cast by the morning sun. One of these dreams revealed itself shortly after Sean's passing.

I'm in Port Elizabeth, with Marcia. We're sorting through boxes we left in storage. We have lots of time. Our flight back to Toronto doesn't leave until 5:30.

The storage room is dark and moldy, the cardboard boxes water-stained.

Marcia holds up a blue sweater and pokes her finger through a hole. The moths got there before us.

I sift through old sneakers, sweatshirts, books, a rugby ball, cricket equipment. "Looks like there's nothing here."

"Look what I found," Marcia says. "A photo of the boys."

Our four sons, smiling patiently. A stark reminder that now there are only three.

I'm suddenly worried about the departure time. I pull the airline confirmation from my black leather bag. "Wait, it says 12:30, not 5:30 p.m." I was certain we were scheduled for a 5:30 flight. "There's no point in trying to phone the airline. I'll be put on hold forever."

On our way to the storeroom, I see a travel agency's neon sigh. If I rush to their office, I can check our departure time.

I stride four blocks in the hot sun. No sign of the travel agency. I must be heading in the wrong direction.

An elderly man is stooped in front of a store window. "Is there a travel agency nearby?" I ask.

"No idea," he says. "I never travel."

A woman mounting her bicycle shakes her head. "There's no

travel agent around here."

I'm confused. Better race back to the storeroom and drive our rental car to the airport.

I take a shortcut through an office building. I enter the front door, expecting it to lead to the other side, nearer to the storeroom, but the corridor darkens. I run frantically along a never-ending carpeted passage, a maze closing in on me. Finally, I find the exit.

Back at the storeroom, Marcia is sitting on one of the boxes, patiently waiting.

"I couldn't find the travel agent," I pant. "I was sure I'd seen a sign." I sound foolish, and now we've missed the plane.

I woke up and lay quietly, eyes closed, amazed at the vivid details of the dream. I wondered how we managed to get the flight back home. I would never know—the dream was over.

But what did it mean? I tried to unravel its message.

My return to our previous hometown could represent a reassessment of my life. The items in the water-stained cardboard boxes, the material possessions, were all worthless now. What held meaning was the photo of the boys. That was the real value of treasured memories.

The dream held other reminders, too. How thoughts and emotions that seemed under control could erupt and shake me to the core. How I feel surefooted one minute and confused the next. And how the journey, interrupted, goes on.

Another dream:

The country road veers to the left, past a red brick wall. I turn the steering wheel, but it's stuck. I tug hard. The wheel is locked. My foot hits the floorboard as I stand on the brakes. The car doesn't stop. I yank the handbrake and it lifts as if disconnected. I frantically pump the brake, pulling at the wheel with one hand and the handbrake with the other, bracing my body for the crash.

I wake up, and relief surges through me.

I couldn't stop the car. It had a mind of its own.

I thought of Sean, taking his life without alerting anyone. Unstoppable.

I'm travelling on a train to an airport. The train is slow; it stops at every station. My friend Solly is with me. (He was my dentist in Port Elizabeth, and I was his lawyer. Together we owned a small farm outside the city, where we kept three riding horses and a few cows, planted vegetables and indulged our fantasy of being farmers.)

"Why is it taking so long?" I ask.

"I don't know. Maybe the airport is far away," Solly answers.

At the next small siding, I get off to stretch my legs. I'm walking along the gravel platform when the shrill whistle sounds and the train jerks forward.

Solly shouts, his hand outstretched. "Jump on! Jump!"

I'm too stunned to jump, and the train rumbles out of the station. As it recedes into the distance, I pat my pocket. It's flat, my wallet with cash and credit cards still in the carriage. I'm overwhelmed. I don't know what to do.

I look around. There's no one on the platform. Parked across the road is a black, early-model Mercedes Benz. A balding elderly man sits in the driver's seat. I walk over, my shoes crunching on the gravel. He looks up from his newspaper.

"My train pulled away. I'm stranded." I wonder if he'll believe my implausible story.

He laughs, and pushes his reading glasses up to his forehead. "No problem. It's a slow train, we'll catch up. Get in the car." He beckons to the passenger seat and sticks out his hand. "I'm Johan." His name and accent tell me he's from South Africa. "You got me at the right time. I'm about to visit a patient—a horse with a sprained leg."

We drive along the country road, past fields and farmhouses. "It's lunch time," he says. "We can grab a quick bite at my house." I doubt there's time for lunch, but I'm in his hands. He stops outside the wrought-iron gates of a large red-brick Victorian-style house. "You can meet my son as well—if he's awake."

The man leads me to the kitchen table laden with a loaf of white bread, sliced turkey and cheese sandwiches. His son comes in. He's pale, rumpled, unshaven, as if he just got up.

"What do you do?" the son asks.

"I'm a litigation lawyer." I consider it discreet not to ask him what he does.

He looks inquiringly at his father. "Dad," he says. "Maybe I should become a lawyer."

His father nods absently. I have a feeling the son will not achieve that goal.

Johan rises from his chair. "We'd better get going if we're going to catch that train."

He drives at a fast clip and we soon reach the train at a small station down the line.

"Thank you so much," I say. "I don't know what I would've done." I'm overwhelmed by his generosity.

"You were in a spot," he smiles. "I had to help you. You seemed desperate."

The Mercedes drives away, and I wake up.

I squeezed my eyes shut to capture each detail and interpret as best I could. I felt that the train portrayed death—Sean's interrupted journey—and the shock of its finality. I was left, helpless to stop it, on the station platform. However, joining up with the train again offered hope of some continuance. The car ride, linked to my South African roots, reflected the spontaneous kindness received from strangers at life's toughest moments.

Each person in the dream had special significance for me. The son brought home Sean's striving to find his own meaningful career.

He had once told me, "I'm thinking, maybe I should do law."

"Sounds like a good idea," I said. Yet I had felt disheartened, knowing that it wasn't likely to happen.

When Solly shouted from the moving train, "Jump on," and stretched out his hand to me, it spoke of the strength of enduring friendships, a source of encouragement when needed.

I was pleased that I caught up with the train in my dream. Its sudden departure didn't mean the end of our journey. At the same time, missing the train also laid bare my powerlessness to manage all of life's events.

I came away from the dream with some hope for the future and a degree of acceptance that Sean was no longer with us.

Marcia woke me. She was sitting bolt upright in bed.

"What's the matter?"

"I walked into a room," she said. "It was all white. Sean was sitting in a chair. I was excited to see he was still alive. A pretty Korean woman was standing on a ladder, putting a book on a high shelf. The woman smiled at me, but Sean looked angry. I asked him where he'd been. He didn't answer. I asked him to please come to our house, but he didn't move."

We spoke about the dream. The lingering hope that flickered in us that maybe somewhere, in another realm, his spirit was still alive.

In waking life, Sean had kept his relationship with the woman he had called "his friend" away from us, yet in the dream, Marcia found them together. We had respected his reasons, whatever they were. We hoped he'd be happy that we had found his friend, that she had become part of the family circle.

Dreams cannot be arbitrarily summoned. They overtake us unexpectedly and tap into our deepest feelings. Waking and sleeping, my dream experiences flitted in and out of my consciousness. They insisted on their own reality and demanded my attention. It was as if the presence of Sean's absence kept recurring. Marcia and I discussed our dreams and questioned their many signposts, seeking clues that might guide us along our future paths.

NINETEEN

The Barrydale Dedication

The email from Basil Jones in South Africa was a surprise. The Barrydale parade, he wrote, would be dedicated to Sean. Three months had passed since he had taken his life. A public dedication to him would mean a great deal to us, especially at this time. Moved by the parade committee's gesture, Marcia and I decided to attend. Despite the long flights, we needed to be there.

History, however, had other plans for that date.

Basil Jones and Adrian Kohler were the founders of the Handspring Puppet Company, creators of the puppets for the internationally acclaimed *War Horse,* the stage play originally produced by the National Theatre of Great Britain. The play, based on the novel by Michael Mopurgo, was about Joey, a horse sent off to the First World War, and his owner, Albert.

Handspring had also co-produced with William Kentridge, the celebrated South African artist, *Ubu and the Truth Commission, Faustus in Africa,* and *Woyzeck on the Highveld.*

The Barrydale Giant Puppet Parade and Performance, which started in 2010, had become a landmark creative event involving hundreds of participants from the local community, especially the youth, as performers, artists, musicians, and puppeteers. Together with other groups, Handspring offered workshops in puppetry, dance, and music to the impoverished inhabitants of the village, all of whom contributed to this festive annual event.

Sean had helped raise funds in Toronto for the parade. The board's decision to honour him at the parade was also a genuine expression of sympathy for our loss.

A few days before we were to leave Toronto for Cape Town, Nelson Mandela was taken off life support. South Africa, like the rest of the world, openly grieved his death by taking time out to recall his values, his humanity, and his extraordinary achievements. It was a momentous time to be returning to our former home country. The funeral was scheduled for Sunday, the same day as the parade; we understood this to mean the latter would likely be postponed for a few days, or even cancelled.

Mandela was Sean's hero. A major highlight of the time we spent in South Africa with him and Danusia was his visit to Mandela's prison cell on Robben Island.

And there were other associations with Mandela. My chest tightened each time I remembered the two dolls Sean had chosen as his companions, at the end. The one of Mandela, in his unmistakable Madiba shirt, could have been Sean's last image as he took his own life.

We called Basil to ask the obvious. "Is the parade still on?"

"We're waiting," he said, "for a decision."

We flew overnight from Toronto to London, then overnight from London to Cape Town, all on the off-chance that the event would proceed as planned.

We were in Cape Town, on the Friday, when Basil called about the parade. "I'm sorry," he said. "It will probably be postponed because of the funeral."

The news did not come as a surprise. Everyone around the globe would be watching the funeral on television. It made sense to postpone the parade. Even so, it was hard not to feel disappointed.

The entire week before the funeral saw an outpouring of grief on a global scale. Non-stop television programs celebrated Madiba's remarkable life. Newspapers carried articles about his life and times. The largest group of dignitaries ever to assemble were expected to congregate in South Africa to attend his funeral.

Basil called again. "The children and the community worked hard to prepare for the parade; it will be held on Monday night."

We didn't care whether it was on Sunday or Monday night; we were just happy it was going ahead.

A few days later, another phone call from Basil. "The committee has decided that it will take place late Sunday afternoon, after the funeral."

We were amazed at the coincidence that Sean would be honoured on the day of the funeral. I imagined him smiling, saying, "Wow."

The long months that Mandela had been on life support, nearly six in all, had been a busy time in preparation for mourning rituals. Opportunists used the celebration of his life to their advantage. The president of South Africa, Jacob Zuma, and his fellow party members hoped to bask in the limelight and elevate themselves in the glow of Mandela's renown. Mandela was revered as a statesman who forgave his enemies and jailers; he was a man who fought for peace and reconciliation. His legacy served to highlight the corruption of some of his successors in the African National Congress—an irony lost on most of them.

President Zuma appeared in front of the cameras and was loudly booed. The eyes of the world were upon him. In South Africa, however, the broadcasting corporation excised the embarrassing spectacle from their programs.

As the day of the funeral approached, despots of the world jetted into South Africa, accompanied by sizeable entourages. Politicians and political operators who paid only lip service to Mandela's values sought to burnish their tarnished images on the world's stage.

Watching the funeral on television, I was confounded by the erratic hand gestures of the sign language interpreter standing next to Barack Obama. Later, I read that murder charges had been laid against the interpreter, but they could not proceed as he had to be admitted to a psychiatric hospital. The lack of proper security was just one more indication of the ineptitude of the ANC-controlled government right down to preparations for the funeral.

I watched the television closely, thinking about the upcoming parade. What would be said, I wondered, in the dedication to Sean?

We drove to Barrydale with Jane Taylor, a distinguished academic who became our navigator and who, in many ways, eased the emotional intensity of the two-and-a-half-hour journey by exploring with us our shared interests.

Starting out in Cape Town, we drove past Groote Schuur Hospital, where the world's first heart transplant had taken place. I reminded Marcia of Frumilla, the person I'd once dated who had gone on to become part of that pioneering transplant team. She smiled, remembering we had met through my phone call to Frumilla.

Jane told us, "I wrote a mystery involving a heart transplant." She later gave me a copy of *The Transplant Men*." It involved a mysterious death, an organ recipient, and the heart transplant pioneer Dr. Chris Barnard. I opened the book to the striking first sentence: "Each suicide is unique." How well I understood the many facets of that statement.

The long drive sped by. On the N2 route, we passed Langa and the corrugated iron-and-board shacks with their hundreds of outhouses lining the road. A country of stunning scenic beauty clashed with a vast, ever-widening chasm between the wealth of a few and the abject poverty of many.

We marvelled at the spectacular views as we drove through Sir Lowry's Pass and Houwhoek Pass where dark clouds cast shadows over the landscape. At the historic Tradouw Pass, we snaked over striking mountain landscapes, through narrow winding gorges and around craggy sandstone outcrops. We passed through the Tradouw Valley, renowned for its year-round vineyards and orchards.

We saw wildlife, too. A small troop of grey baboons appeared roadside, and as I slowed down they stared at us, unafraid, before loping away slowly, tails held high. A black eagle soared high above, and we watched until it disappeared.

Everything on the journey made an impression, a fact that was not lost on me. "We very much appreciate Adrian and Basil arranging for today's parade to be dedicated to Sean," I said.

Jane smiled. "It's going to be special. I'm looking forward to hearing what they say."

Marcia and I nodded.

Finally, we arrived in Barrydale, a village of 3,500. Founded in the eighteenth century, Barrydale is lodged between two geographic extremes that lie only ten kilometres apart. On the one side is the fertile Tradouw Valley, and on the other, the semi-arid Klein Karoo. The village was divided in two, to keep Whites separate from "non-Whites." The latter lived in the township of Smitsville, known locally to its inhabitants as *Steek My Weg*, which translates as "Hide Me Away."

It was December 16, the Day of Reconciliation. The activities scheduled for the afternoon and evening brought the community, divided during apartheid, together.

We headed straight for the former Coloured school, the centre of the activities. There Basil and Adrian and young volunteers were stitching sheets that would stimulate waves for tonight's performance. Large, colourful posters advertising the event plastered the walls of the school, prominently acknowledging the Blumberg Family Foundation's contribution. We were there, however, to acknowledge Sean.

When the time came, Marcia and I joined the parade of villagers and tourists that followed the two life-sized elephant puppets. Half the procession, behind one lumbering creature, hived off to the Coloured section of the town and the other half headed to the White area, to later join up at the school.

The large grey puppet with its sparkling white tusks towered above me. Its large ears wiggled, its tail wagged and its trunk moved up and down. Now and then a deafening blast from a plastic vuvuzela, often heard at South African football stadiums, erupted in competition with that of the elephant's trumpeting.

I followed the small procession, led by a band and bugler, avoiding the small pools of water that had collected from the earlier rain shower. A pleasant, musky aroma wafted up from the damp soil. Exhilarated by the excitement of the revellers, I imbibed the festive spirit and imagined the delight that Sean, too, would have felt had he taken part.

At the same time, I felt the void of his absence acutely.

Villagers on their porches laughed and cheered as the gigantic elephant puppet and the band passed their houses. A sudden downpour did not dampen the exuberance of either participants or spectators.

I captured every moment of the event on my video camera to savour and later share with the family in Toronto.

The sun shone through gaps in the dark clouds, making the brightly painted houses of Smitsville appear picturesque. Yet behind the colourful facades beloved by tourists, as we later learned, were residents suffering from drug and alcohol abuse. They were trapped in this rural village and saw their children grow up with no chance of escape.

After the street parade, on raised benches on one side of the local school's playing field, we joined eager spectators from the Coloured township to await the post-parade performance of "When the Sea Comes to the Karoo." Many of the local inhabitants had never seen the sea. We were curious what they would say in dedicating the parade to Sean.

A girl walked by, sucking a pacifier. She looked about seven years of age. Jane whispered to me, "fetal alcohol syndrome."

Many of the young men and women had sunken cheeks, and their smiles revealed missing teeth. The village had neither a dentist nor a doctor, only a clinic. The men who greeted us with exaggerated friendliness were either drunk or high.

A young boy came up to me and beckoned that he wanted to take pictures with my camera. As I showed him how to do so, he lost interest and ran off. Later, during the performance, he darted around the stage and had to be led away. In the village there would be little, if any, help for his behavioural problems.

Even this brief exposure to such challenges made it clear why Basil and Adrian and the Handspring Trust were so important to the community. They trained young people in the creative arts and offered skills that could open doors to further education. Sean would have been happy to see that his fundraising efforts were making hope tangible for young people in a disadvantaged village a world away.

The master of ceremonies walked to the microphone on the small stage. He wore a black suit and a bow tie, with a tartan shawl draped across his shoulders. His hair was plastered down and shaped Mohawk-style. He thanked the volunteers and called on a local priest to bless the crowd in Afrikaans.

When he took over again, I held my breath. Now would be the time to mention Sean.

The MC thanked contributors to the event, including the Blumberg Foundation. Then he said, "We dedicate this parade to the memory of Madiba."

Sean was never mentioned. I was stunned. Marcia and I hadn't come to Barrydale to be thanked for our contribution. We had come because of Sean.

"He could at least have mentioned Sean, even if it was dedicated to Madiba," I whispered to Marcia.

She looked at me with a furrowed brow.

Children swarmed the ground in front of the stage, waving sheets and hoisting colourful goldfish made out of plastic bags. A large, brightly coloured mermaid puppet rose from the waves. I watched the performance, dazed, and lost all track of the storyline. We had travelled from Canada to be present at the dedication. Why had Sean's name not been mentioned at all?

Afterwards, Adrian walked briskly our way. He gave us both a big hug. "It was agreed that Basil would have a chance to speak, and he was going to mention Sean." Adrian was bordering on tears. "The master of ceremonies didn't give him a chance." He reassured us, "Sean will be mentioned on our website."

Marcia and I looked at one another. We would have to overcome this disappointment.

That evening we joined volunteers at the Dung Beetle restaurant, where we met Peter Takelo, a man who had dedicated his life to uplifting children in the village and surrounding farms. Peter was one of the founders of Net Vir Pret, meaning Just for Fun.

"What does Net Vir Pret do?" I asked.

Peter led me to a quiet corner of the room and explained that the group worked with children facing poverty, alcoholism, drug abuse, domestic violence and teenage pregnancy. During the school holidays, the organization also offered programs to occupy the children creatively.

I imagined Sean sitting next to me, leaning forward in rapt attention.

Fruit pickers and labourers were paid about 125 rand a day, Peter said. I was shocked. That was around twelve dollars a day, barely enough for a quarter tank of gas for our hired car—or a few loaves of bread. Some workers also had to pay for electricity in their rental cottages out of their meagre wages. It was then that I better understood the suffering inside the colourful cottages. The towns, and the wine and fruit farms, were filled with people facing not just enormous challenges but sheer desperation.

In situations of poverty, children bear the brunt of hardship.

Basil and Adrian joined us for dinner. They had spoken to the master of ceremonies, who said he'd forgotten that the event was to be dedicated to Sean. "What is important," Basil said in a quiet voice, "is that Sean is in our hearts." Marcia and I knew that was so.

After the ceremony, we checked the Handspring Puppet Trust website. The video of the parade ended with the statement, "This film is dedicated to the memory of Sean Blumberg 1976-2021." There was also an acknowledgment: "Our major sponsor this year was the Blumberg Family Trust. Marcia and Henry Blumberg live and work in Toronto."

More significant for us was the personal dedication. "Sean's untimely passing last year was a great, great loss to the Blumberg family. Basil and Adrian personally dedicated their work on this parade to the memory of this sweet and generous man."

Reading these lines, I took a deep breath. I hoped that somehow, somewhere, Sean would be aware of those words, especially as they were written by two men whom he admired and whose work excited and inspired him.

A few weeks later we visited Adrian and Basil's studio in Kalk Bay, a suburb of Cape Town. We had mentioned that we would love to have something of their work. Adrian suggested Emilie, the only puppet they had made to play a French child of war in the production of *War Horse*; the role was later filled by an actor.

"If you or your children ever have to part with her," Basil said, "she can't be sold. She must go to a museum."

There, in the studio, we watched Emilie's creator gently wrap the puppet. Adrian had lovingly carved her. Now she would begin her journey with us to her new home in Canada. We were excited at this further bond with special friends and happy to continue our support of the work of the Handspring Foundation.

We were moved at their generosity. The puppet Emilie held great significance for us. We had seen her in the original National Theatre production of *War Horse*. Her war-weary face evokes the terrible fate and horrors of children trapped in combat. Tragically, the real Emilie on whom the puppet is based did not survive the war. Her grandfather had written that he did not want her to be "just a name on a gravestone that no one will read." He had wanted her story remembered.

How well we knew that yearning, for a loved one to be remembered.

That's what we wanted for Sean, that he not be forgotten.

Back in Cape Town, where we were staying with Marcia's aunt Irma, we told her of the dedicated volunteers we'd met. Her comment brought us up short. "It must have been hard when they mentioned Sean."

We said nothing. There was no point in saying that it was harder that Sean had not been mentioned.

We remembered the excitement on the faces of the villagers during the performance as they applauded their children's participation and everyone they recognized among the performers.

On Sunday the world had viewed the funeral of Madiba and acknowledged his altruism to make the world a better place for all, especially children. It was also the day we truly understood the value of Sean's contribution to help a few children in a distant village he had never seen to break free of their cycle of poverty.

In our hearts, and to those who knew him, the parade had also been dedicated to Sean. It didn't have to be announced. Sean was our son and we were proud that, despite his own struggle, he strove to make the world a better place. The hope lighting up the children's faces on stage was enough. Sean would not have asked for more.

TWENTY

Reunited

Three years had passed and still I yearned to reach out to Sean's spirit, feel his presence, and comprehend his feelings in taking his life. A void persisted that I needed to fill.

I was hoping, although not really believing, that somehow, through some mystical intervention, we could reconnect with Sean.

Marcia felt the same way, and suggested we visit a spiritual medium. After some inquiries, we were referred to one.

Sandy lived near Georgetown, a short drive west of Toronto. She had become a medium after her daughter died in a car crash.

I was skeptical about working with a medium, but after some vacillation, I called and got this message on her answering machine: "I have a two-year waiting list. Please don't leave a message unless you are a bereaved parent."

Those last two words qualified us.

On the appointed day, as we whizzed by factories and warehouses along Highway 401, I felt a pang of recognition. I pictured Sean driving us to Pearson International Airport. That was the last time we saw him.

Marcia said softly, "Wherever Sean is, I hope he's not alone and is with family."

I felt a cold shiver, thinking of Sean moving between strange, dark worlds on his own. My hands gripped the steering wheel as I focused on the stream of cars ahead. My emotions careened from doubting that we would connect with him to a faint hope that we would, although I couldn't imagine what such a communication would mean. Part of me dreaded what might unfold in the medium's presence, yet I knew this was a path I had to pursue.

The sky turned overcast and raindrops splattered the windshield. The factories and warehouses gave way to green fields and the occasional farmhouse. As we exited the highway, I remembered Sandy's instructions about the village. "If you blink, you'll miss it." We peered at every house number on the street until we found her single-storey brick home set well back from the road.

Sandy welcomed us at the door with a friendly smile. She was casually dressed. We had only given her our first names; she didn't enquire more about us. She led us to a small study with a two-seater couch. The curtains were partly drawn. Placing an old black tape recorder on the coffee table, she took a seat opposite us. "I'll give you a copy of the tape at the end."

Sandy lowered her eyes and her face changed, her smile fading to a frown.

Is this what a trance looks like? I wondered.

Questions kept surfacing while I waited for her to speak. Was Sean in contact with deceased family members? There were my parents, Julius and Ida; Marcia's parents, Scott and Doreen; and our granddaughter, his niece, Sasha Bella. Sean had loved her deeply. I thought of the joy he had missed in not being part of the lives of his nephews and nieces as they grew up and transformed from adorable babies to teenagers and mature adults. I also wondered if he regretted death by suicide.

The medium spoke. “There’s an older man coming through who wants to talk to you. He’s going to run the reading. It could be your dad.” Sandy touched her chest. “He could have suffered a heart attack. He passed suddenly and didn’t say goodbye.”

I feel a bursting inside. Could she really see my dad? She was right about his heart attack and my being too late to see him. Maybe it was just a lucky guess. Many people die of heart attacks.

“He’s in front of a group. There’s also a baby.”

I was curious about the group. Was Sean among them?

“Your dad’s presenting as a younger man. I can’t tell if he was in his fifties or seventies when he died.” She smiled. “He wants to be young.”

I was not convinced that the figure was Dad.

She stared at me. “What’s the J connection?”

I was stunned. Dad’s name was Julius. That “J” couldn’t be a lucky guess. The connection had an odd effect on me. I suddenly felt like an intruder, peering through a peephole into a forbidden world far beyond the living.

“Your mom passed away too. She’s letting your dad handle the reading. Both of them have always been there for you.”

I nodded. Despite my skepticism, I felt a wave of relief that they were with us.

“Your dad cries for you,” Sandy said to me. “He missed a lot of your life, your children and grandchildren, but he’s been around you.”

It was true that Dad had not met Marcia, let alone our sons and nine grandchildren.

In my mind’s eye I saw an image: a black-and-white photo of Dad as a dashing young man striding down a street, snapped by a photographer in Johannesburg.

I felt a measure of foreboding as she closed her eyes. What would she say next?

"There's a young man with your dad. There's an S in his name. Maybe an SN, a Simon or Samson."

Marcia's jaw dropped. We hadn't given Sandy Sean's name or any information about him.

She continued, "The young man next to your dad could be the son that you are mourning. He dealt with lots of emotional issues. There was depression and medication he should have taken, and didn't." The medium opened her eyes and spoke slowly. "Your dad was with him as he struggled. He helped your son. He found him quickly and was there to get him. He didn't leave alone."

I choked up, picturing Dad gently lifting Sean from the chair, holding his hand as they both drifted away.

"It could be your son died by suicide, but I'm not sure yet. Your dad's waiting for him to tell me himself or give me some sign."

She looked down again. "Yes, your son died by suicide. My sign is his head is down. He is taking responsibility. Someone always brings them on. That's what your dad did." She took a deep breath. "I feel your son can't breathe. This is definitely a suicide."

We had not told her how Sean died.

"I'll wait for your son to communicate. They are trying to show the scene of how he was found. Your son says it didn't hurt. There was no blood." She shifted in her chair. The light in the room seemed to darken. "He says, 'I did this before.' Another attempt. He keeps showing me a bathroom. He tried to do something before with blood. Later there was the breathing, the gas I felt at the beginning. Your dad acknowledges he was there for the first one with blood. He's showing me a suicide scene, in the bathroom."

I saw on Marcia's face how she relived the horror of seeing the scar on Sean's neck. He said he hadn't meant it seriously, that it was "a gesture." While he had tried to lessen our fears, we remained alarmed that he had even considered taking his own life.

The medium continued. "Your dad couldn't stop him. Nobody could stop him. It's important you know that."

The words "nobody could stop him" were heartbreaking. They were also reassuring.

A puzzled look crossed Sandy's face. "I sense there is something he left undone."

Right away, I knew what she meant. Sean had left neither a suicide note nor a message for the person he had called his "friend." We had been the ones to contact her, to tell her of his death. She had driven with us to the cemetery, in the funeral limousine.

"His head is down. He's hanging onto your father. It means he's saying, 'I'm sorry.' Your son is now telling me you were out of the country when it happened … He's extending his arm, he's taking responsibility. He couldn't get out of this black hole. His emotional issues went on for years. He's now facing them. He was taken over by this illness. Suicide generally isn't the answer, but at the time he wasn't well."

Sandy paused. "With my daughter, it was different. She was twenty-two. She died in a car crash. It wasn't her fault."

We nodded and appreciated Sandy sharing her own painful journey.

"We don't get over it," she said. "It's been sixteen years. We still miss her, and our unborn grandchildren, but we've learned to cope. I didn't stay the same crazy person I was for eighteen months after it happened. They also want you to find joy."

At the outset the trauma had shocked us into an almost automaton-like mode.

She looked down again, as if in a trance. "Your son makes me feel he is with you. You have to trust him. It's never ever going to be enough because you want him back. He's there. If you feel him near, you're not crazy. He's around you."

She lifted her chin. "This reading is important to him. He's telling you he's sorry. This will help all of you, but it can't fix what happened."

A parent forever carries the sadness of a child's death, especially if death comes by their own hand.

"Your son loves you a lot. It was never lack of love, you helped him enough. It wasn't about you. He couldn't get his head right. He's learning now on the other side. Your dad has helped him. He feels the grief he caused you."

The words "the grief he caused" resonated deeply. Marcia and I had always been acutely aware of one thing: parents can only be as happy as their unhappiest child.

Grief from loss flows in many directions. There is the grief he feels he caused us. There is our pain in the face of his absence. There is our mourning the abrupt ending of his youthful dreams. There is the ongoing grief of knowing that his bright hopes and aspirations will remain forever unfulfilled.

"There isn't a ring on his finger. He never married. He was an adult. You looked after him in some way; he is touching his heart in thanks. He always appreciated everything you did for him." She looked directly at us. "He needs you to hear you did everything you could for him."

Marcia squeezed my hand.

The balm for grief is gratitude.

Sandy leaned forward and furrowed her brow. "There is another M there, for sure. An older man."

"My grandfather on my mother's side was Mendel," I said.

She shook her head. "No. There is also an R."

"It can't be Marcia's Dad, he was called Scott," I said. I had no idea what the M might mean.

Marcia smiled broadly. "He's my father. His real name was Meyer. Scott was his nickname."

True. How had I missed that?

Sandy nodded. "He's here. He is smiling and thanking you for easing his passing. He was in hospital. You put on a nurse's cap even though you're not a nurse. You helped him at the end of his life."

Again, all true.

"Your mother is here too," Sandy told Marcia. "Did she pass away from cancer? She wants you to know she's been there for you. When your parents moved here, you were still there. You rushed over to see her at the end. She thanks you for being with her."

Marcia's eyes brimmed with tears. She had rushed from South Africa to Toronto to be with her mother as she lay dying within a few weeks after arriving in Canada.

Marcia's voice broke as she told Sandy that Doreen had hidden her symptoms in South Africa. She had avoided going to a doctor till she arrived in Canada, afraid it would delay their immigration.

Whenever I think of Doreen, I am moved by her selfless act. I know that Marcia is touched even more so by her mother's sacrifice. Doreen would never be able to delight in the joys of her grandchildren or great-grandchildren, as yet unborn.

"Your son is with her too," Sandy said, "and she's caring for him. You did a lot for her. She says you went through enough, did enough, and saw her enough. She's dancing around your head and walks with you. So, talk to your father and mother. Perhaps this will comfort you. Your son is getting the help he needs from your family.

"Another man is rocking a little one. I can't tell if it's a girl or a boy. There is some pink. Is there a little girl who died? I hear a name Isabelle or Bella, or such name as that. She was born really sick. I feel there is an important birthday today."

Marcia gasped and raised her hand to her mouth. "It's her birthday today, June 6th. Her name is Sasha Bella. She would've been ten today. We're going to Jonathan and Pam's for dinner to symbolically cut her birthday cake."

"Oh my gosh." A look of amazement lit up Sandy's face. Then, a sudden frown. "What is the black-and-white dog connection please? You don't have a dog?"

I told her we had a beautiful small black cat with a patch of white on her chest.

Sandy shook her head.

Then I remembered Sam, who belonged to Jonathan and Pam. Sasha used to play with him. He would sniff around her, waiting for her to throw him a scrap of food. She'd gurgle with impish delight, watching him gobble it up. Then he'd stare fixedly again, with pleading eyes, hoping for another morsel.

I saw an image of Sean standing next to Sasha Bella, laughing.

"There's somebody with Sasha," Sandy said. "A name with a B in it. It could be a BR or Boris."

Marcia said it couldn't be Sasha's three-year-old brother, Bram; he was still alive.

The medium nodded. "It has to be somebody on the other side."

"There's a November birthday your dad hasn't forgotten. Is it yours?"

I nodded, amazed that Dad remembered.

"These details are to prove it's him talking to me. It's his way of saying, 'I'm running this reading. I'm helping.' That's all he can do. I don't understand anything. I just give."

She abruptly changed the subject. "Did you have an operation?"

Before I could reply, she said, "It wasn't your time. He knows you got a cleaning out of valves, or a new one. Your dad was with you, watching you." I shivered, realizing how fortunate I was to be alive. Dad might have intervened on my behalf. My recovery from my double bypass and aortic valve replacement had indeed been spectacular. Marcia said that each night before retiring, she had looked at Sean's photo on her computer screen and said, "Seanie, look after Henry, please." In some mystical, incomprehensible manner, maybe Dad and Sean had both helped me.

Sandy turned to Marcia. "Henry's dad is acknowledging you as a loving daughter. Have you met him?"

He would have admired Marcia for the way she raised our sons. She was a role model for our grandchildren and a loving, supportive spouse. She had courageously dealt with the loss of a beloved granddaughter and son. Despite all of that, she had become a respected and compassionate university professor.

"You learned much from your dad," Sandy told me.

I nodded. Whenever he thought I was being headstrong, he would say, "I want to give you the benefit of my experience." I smiled inwardly, recalling Dad's folksy sayings. *A fool and his money are soon parted. When you lend, you lose a friend. Nothing ventured, nothing gained.*

"He is proud of you, by the way."

I choked up. Maybe he knew far more than I'd imagined: the choices we'd made, the obstacles we'd worked so hard to overcome. Dad used to say that every family carried its own *peckel*, the burden borne while striving to keep walking, to keep moving forward.

I now understood more fully what he meant.

Then I thought of something else. Perhaps he was proud of my persistence in trying to discover what had happened to his family during the Holocaust. Having witnessed Dad's anguish throughout the war and its aftermath, I had made it my mission to trace any and all survivors. I had travelled to Latvia many times. I'd researched archives there as well as in Israel, Germany, South Africa and the United States. I had scrolled through hundreds of websites and search engines, searching, over many years, for the answer to the haunting question: What had happened to his parents, my grandparents, Jacob and Ernestine and our family in Latvia?

I found the chilling truth. The family had been brutally executed, thrown into mass graves. Dad had lost his parents, brothers, sister, cousins—his immediate family were all gone.

Yet I managed to find three cousins who had miraculously survived the horrors of Stutthof and the Bergen-Belsen concentration camp. I also discovered extended family who had escaped Latvia in time.

I understood now that Dad was healing, embracing Sasha Bella and comforting and guiding Sean.

"Do you write?" Sandy asked. "He's at your back when you're writing."

I nodded, surprised.

For three years I'd been trying to transform a torrent of emotions into words. I struggled to portray the many facets of his grandson; some sparkling and delightful; others witty and endearing; others still darkened by depression and anxiety. My writing helped me to recover my voice and come to terms with changes in myself as well.

Sometimes, when I sat at my desk to read what my fingers had created the previous day on my iPad keyboard, the thoughts and wells of feeling surprised me. While my writing journey has navigated rapids and reefs, I felt compelled to continue because of my self-revelatory experience.

Sandy fell quiet for a short while. She then looked directly at Marcia and me. "Someone came looking for your son and knocked on his door. A brother found him. Your son cries for him. He knows he is struggling and at times it affects the family."

Kevin had torn the helium mask off Sean's face. I understood Sean crying for his brother, not wanting him to have to live with the horror of that experience.

"Somebody living has an AL link, an Alice or Alish. It has to do with the brother who found him." Sandy looked at us, expecting an answer.

Marcia covered her mouth in amazement.

"Alisa. Kevin's wife was there as well," I said.

"Was there a Katherine there? Your dad acknowledges a Kate or Kathy. There's also an M connection. He's taking me close to the person who found him."

Kevin and Alisa's three children, Kate, Matthew and Julian. were in the car. They heard the screech of the sirens and watched the burly police officers and paramedics dash by, not knowing the cause of the turmoil.

"Your son is making me feel how it was when his brother came and couldn't help him. He was already with your dad, on the other side. There is a John, Johnny. Your son hugs him too."

That would be Jonathan, our firstborn and Sean's oldest brother.

"Did he work in the family business? Your son left a lot of

heaviness on Johnny's shoulders, and he wants to talk about Johnny's kids. Are there three girls?"

She was right. There were three girls: Sasha Bella who passed away, Mia and Evie. And their brother, Bram.

"I see the letters MR."

"Mark," Marcia said.

Mark was the last brother to see Sean alive. He'd reached out to Sean on the Saturday, a week before he died, to discuss a law office website project both were working on to provide greater clarity on Canadian registered charities. The Sean Blumberg Transparency Project has assisted over 86,000 Canadian non-profits and charities to be more transparent, legal, ethical and effective.

Jonathan, Kevin and Mark were all caring brothers. Each of them had invited Sean to join them at different times during the last week of his life, the week we were in Edinburgh. He had thanked them, but he'd also refused them. It was clear to us afterwards. He had made up his mind. Nothing and no one were going to stop him.

Sandy looked directly at me. "Your dad is smiling in my head. You must talk to him. Don't feel uncomfortable talking to him out loud."

I imagined Dad standing there, looking at me. Somehow, in an indefinable way, I knew that he and Mom were hovering around us, unseen, watching over the family.

"None of this makes any logical sense," Sandy said. "You have to trust all the different signs; nothing will be as big or as perfect as you want it. They're all together and your dad's handling it. It's good for him as well."

I promised myself I would reach out to them in my quiet moments: times of reflection in my study, or at the cottage as I looked out at the lake and the ducks waddling on the lawn, the Canada Geese overhead, and as I paddled my canoe silently along the rippling water's edge.

"There is now a pullback," Sandy told us. "Your family do not stay with me; they came with you and return home with you."

She got up slowly.

We thanked her.

She led us out of the small room to her front door, where we shook her hand.

Outside, I blinked in the bright sunlight. The unexpected revelations had filled us with a sense of wonder. There was so much to process. We had arrived, in Sandy's words, as "bereaved parents," hoping to connect with Sean. What we had discovered was beyond our dreams. He was sorry. He felt our pain. At the same time, his own had been too great.

And there was more. Sean was with family. He was holding Dad's hand. Dad had taken over from us. He had directed the reading with the family around him. He was there for Sean and Sasha Bella, for us all. That alone was a great consolation.

The initials BR remained unresolved. As we left Sandy's house I wondered if we would ever find out more.

We drove directly to Pam and Jonathan's for dinner, to acknowledge Sasha's birthday. I missed Sasha Bella's bouncy presence in her booster seat, revelling in the family's love and adoration. Today she couldn't blow out the candles, and yet as Jonathan sliced the big, colourful, chocolate birthday cake—her favourite—I sensed the entire family, seen and unseen, gathered round.

We waited until the children were in bed to share our experience with the medium. Jonathan and Pam listened, smiling faintly, as if they were respectfully indulging us.

"One thing we didn't understand," I said. "She spoke of a BR with Sasha Bella. He was the only person I couldn't identify."

Pam stared at us in disbelief. "That's my father, Bruce. He died many years ago."

He was there, then. And why wouldn't he be? Sasha Bella was his granddaughter.

When we finally arrived home after that extraordinary day, I retired to my study and slumped in my armchair to collect my thoughts. I felt drained and exhausted. Behind me, looking over me, was Sean's Ndebele mural.

"We understand why and what you did, Sean," I whispered. "We love you very much and miss you terribly. Thank you for being there and reaching out to us today."

I thanked Dad for his care and the family's support for Sean and Sasha.

I felt certain that they heard me, that we were all together.

My awareness was now heightened in a way I had never before experienced. We had connected with Sean and the family. We could rest assured that they were caring for him and Sasha.

As my thoughts deepened, so too did my breathing. The lingering emptiness I had carried with me was slowly being replaced by an unfamiliar feeling. Serenity.

There, on my desk, were Sean's files and notebooks piled high as they had been for three years. Finally, I felt that I could face them, and delve more deeply into his writing and his drawings.

In the silence I felt a buzzing in my ears. In my mind's eye, I saw Sean standing next to Dad. Behind them, in grey outlines, gathered Sasha and other family members.

Three long years had dragged by as I'd struggled to find my voice out of grief. I had sat in my study, journeying through my past. I felt grateful that Sean had encouraged my odyssey, my quest to recollect and record his short life.

I came to understand the words of Kierkegaard, the philosopher: "Life must be understood backward, [even though] it is lived forward."

I felt my chair shifting, becoming a canoe.

The sky darkened, the wind rose and the waves grew turbulent. Sean was pulling hard at the paddle, to reach the shore. We hauled the canoe onto muddy ground, then relaxed for a spell before portaging through towering pine, birch, spruce, maple, oak, and elm trees. At times, we felt sure we were lost. Together, we carried the heavy load up and down the narrow pathways, winding between dense shrubs and trees. Eventually, we reached calmer waters, where we could relaunch.

On my skin, I felt a prickly sensation I had never before experienced. I had arrived at another destination.

EPILOGUE

The living cannot fully fathom the finality of death.

I knew that Sean was no longer with us. But knowing is vastly different from grasping the darkness of the void of everlasting sleep. While death by any cause is heartbreaking, the loss of a beloved person to suicide brings with it added layers of emotion for the bereaved, layers that need to be peeled away. I recalled the helplessness we felt at times. Despite all the good memories, despite all our efforts, our interventions to help Sean came to naught.

Past events are embedded in time and cannot be changed. Wisps of memories flashing by reflect imperfectly; they are not an exact mirror of the past. I strove to gather and combine fleeting images into a narrative, a crutch of hope and comfort of remembrances to carry us into the future.

For nine years after Sean's death, I continued writing about him, recalling my memories and those of others. I was delighted to discover the joy he brought to family and friends in his teenage years, before he was gradually overcome by paranoia and depression. As I delved into both our lives, I tried to capture some of his thoughts, hopes, aspirations, fears, happiness, and humour; in so doing, I found that the trajectory of our interwoven beings grew even closer. I gained a greater understanding of who he was and all that he meant to us and embraced, finally, the acceptance that he had left us.

Marcia, my beloved spouse of over fifty years, was the impetus for starting this journey. She asked the challenging question, "What is the single most important thing that has happened to you in the past few years?"

Without a moment's hesitation, I replied, "Sean's death." Marcia's unwavering support and encouragement sustained my endeavour, especially in moments when I floundered in a vortex of conflicting thoughts and emotions.

Time and introspection have provided a measure of consolation.

Now that I'm writing the epilogue about Sean and our family, I realize that I'm reaching the destination of this creative endeavour. Death by suicide never yields closure for the bereaved. For me, it has been important to relive my journey with Sean and to share it. Having experienced the mixture of joyous and unhappy times during my quest, I can now walk with a lighter tread.

In recording the recollections, I discovered the inspiration that helped propel me to pursue my odyssey with Sean.

During the process of my long reflection, I kept sorting through Sean's possessions, including the files, notebooks, a diary that chronicled some of the years up to his mid-twenties, his photos, sketch pads, medical records—all that documented parts of his life.

Poring over those papers surprised and moved me. I admired his perseverance as he vainly fought to overcome the physical pain, depression and intense fears that had engulfed him. In one of his notebooks he also expressed his deep appreciation for acts of kindness received.

I learnt much about him, emotions he never shared with us, but now that I looked closely, I could see everywhere. Parents often know little about the thoughts of their teenage and young adult children.

I continue to respect his striving and in so doing feel greater empathy with the suffering of others, whether through illness, wars, deprivation or the emotional, physical, and financial pain of the Covid-19 pandemic.

In our bereavement, we embraced meaningful acts to help carry us through each successive day. We continue to participate in religious observances, the memorial prayers recited for the deceased during the Day of Atonement and on the eighth day of Passover. We attend services each year on the anniversary of his death when his name is called out. We observe the custom of lighting a candle in our house annually in his honour and recall memories about him as we gaze at his photo prominently displayed among our family photographs.

We have created family rituals that we call "our remembrances": We visit his grave regularly and add to the numerous pebbles on his tombstone. We celebrate his birthday every year with a family dinner and remember to serve his favourite chocolate ice-cream cake with coloured icing balloons. We evoke smiles when we choose lemon grass chicken from the buffet at his favourite Chinese restaurant. Marcia continues to say good night to Sean as she looks at his image on the computer screen before going to sleep. Those are among the bittersweet times when we are so aware of the absence of his presence.

Each of our sons, daughters-in-law, and grandchildren have shared and created their own special memories of Sean whether through Facebook or naming a website in his honour.

My writing and recording of our life with Sean and the exchange of memories have also bonded us as a family.

The thought that keeps recurring is that no one is truly dead until all the memories of that person have faded away.

Many believe that those who die by suicide do not consider the pain borne by their surviving family and friends. People who are suicidal may think that their death will lessen the pain of their parents, by simply cutting life short. While we will never know what Sean thought, he could not have imagined the weight of grief he left behind.

What I now know is that constantly surmising cannot bring us to a satisfying conclusion.

The inspiring musical, *Dear Evan Hansen,* deals with the grief and loneliness endured by a bullied seventeen-year-old boy. It resonated with me about the need for human connection. Its haunting refrain, "You Are Not Alone," reminded me of the comfort provided by family and friends at surprising times and places: the unexpected hug, the sharing of common grief, the unsaid words while the eyes glisten with empathy. I always knew I would have to chart my own path, yet their constant support provided the consolation to carry me through each day.

Marcia and I, in our darkest moments, asked ourselves whether we could have done more. As time passed we came to accept that nothing we did, or could have done, would ultimately have changed the outcome. Still, in quiet moments, there lurks the gnawing thought that in every certainty a touch of uncertainty lingers.

Over time, by delving into his life and our shared experiences, I no longer had to ask "why." I learnt more about his past pain and his many years of striving to escape both depression and paranoia. The only question that remained was, Why then? For a while I speculated. I thought about all that might have caused him to spiral into the depths of despair at the time of his death. But I will never know for certain.

In the process of my discovery and writing, I have learnt much about mental illness and the lingering stigma that still clings to it. Perhaps I have even gained a greater empathy with the general suffering prevalent in society. Despite my greater awareness of this devastating illness, I believe that the agony of the black dog cannot be fully fathomed unless one has personally experienced and grappled with the darkness.

As part of our journey to find solace, Marcia and I needed to reach into Sean's spiritual world. I am pleased that I overcame my initial skepticism about approaching a medium. Marcia and I were surprised by her many revelations and continue to be comforted that Sean's spirit is indeed surrounded by family.

People suffer a loss by suicide in their individual ways. We must chart our own paths to healing, whether through counselling, meditation, writing, sharing and speaking of grief with close friends, or creating acts of remembrance.

And yet, while the wound closes, the scar remains. Today, nine years after Sean's passing, the raw pain has subsided yet there remains a gnawing ache.

I continue to walk, all the while feeling that small pebble of remembrance in my shoe.

Bereavement reveals many of life's lessons. So it has for me. I have accepted that grief is a cost of living. A person who has never experienced deep sorrow has been deprived of an emotional depth of humanity.

I did not want the only tangible remembrance of Sean to be a dark green tombstone in the Pardes Shalom Cemetery outside Toronto. Nor did I want all the wonderful memories of him to be drowned in a sinkhole of oblivion. And we did not want Sean's life to be defined by his act of suicide.

And as I look to the future, I hope that my engagement with Sean over the last nine years, as well as my immense gratitude for our time shared, and finally, my acceptance of the finality of loss through our remembrance, may provide a beacon to others as they navigate through their own darkness to a light that provides solace.

In my mind's eye I can see Sean with a bemused smile saying, "Wow, Henry. You wrote this book about me."

"Yes, Sean. I wrote it because we love and miss you and always want to keep you in our hearts and thoughts."

CPSIA information can be obtained
at www.ICGtesting.com
Printed in the USA
BVHW010857061122
651006BV00014B/19/J

9 781778 138928